LIFT UP YOUR
HEART

"After reading this book, you'll crave holiness in a whole new way and find yourself equipped with time-tested tools for renewing your relationship with God and living a daily life of communion with him."

Cardinal Timothy M. Dolan
Archbishop of New York

"Reading this book is a true retreat—it quickly drew my prayer life to new depths. Fr. John takes us through the timeless wisdom of St. Francis de Sales in a way that is accessible and applicable for anyone at any age. A must-read and a real gift!"

Sarah Swafford
Author of *Emotional Virtue*

"This is an altogether beautiful book filled with wholesome and attractive spiritual wisdom. It presents the spirituality of St. Francis de Sales in a lively, accessible style that is utterly sincere. It should gain the widest possible readership and may very well endure as a small, portable classic in its own right. Highly recommended."

John C. Cavadini
McGrath-Cavadini Director, McGrath Institute for Church Life
University of Notre Dame

"In this book, Fr. John Burns helps us access the famous meditations of St. Francis de Sales in order to put ourselves in the presence of God. This is a gift that ultimately speaks to our salvation and cultivates the daily decisions that help us choose God now and in everything we do. This book is for all who take their faith seriously but somewhere along the way dismissed the notions of heaven and hell. Through his commentary on St. Francis de Sales's themes of judgment and death, heaven and hell, Fr. John Burns reminds us of their centrality to our eternal life and implications for our time here on earth."

Carolyn Woo
Distinguished President's Fellow for Global Development
Purdue University

LIFT UP YOUR
HEART

A 10-DAY PERSONAL RETREAT WITH
ST. FRANCIS DE SALES

John Burns

Based on the Spiritual Classic
Introduction to the Devout Life

AVE MARIA PRESS AVE Notre Dame, Indiana

Nihil Obstat: Reverend Thomas Knoebel
                    Censor Librorum

Imprimatur: +Jerome E. Listecki
                    Archbishop of Milwaukee
                    July 6, 2016

Founded in 1865, Ave Maria Press is a ministry of the United States Province of Holy Cross.

www.avemariapress.com

Paperback: ISBN-13 978-1-59471-720-8

E-book: ISBN-13 978-1-59471-721-5

Cover image of St. Francis de Sales © Julie Lonneman, courtesy of Trinity Stores, www.trinitystores.com, 800.699.4482.

Cover background © iStockphoto.com.

Cover and text design by Katherine J. Ross.

Printed and bound in the United States of America.

Library of Congress Cataloging-in-Publication Data is available.

Contents

To Begin

Like many people, I grew up knowing I was supposed to get to heaven and that God wanted me there. But as a child, I remember not really knowing what heaven *was*, not understanding the supposed goal of my life. With the passing of years, I found less and less attraction to the idea of heaven as it remained something distant, hard to understand, mysterious. With time, I gradually let go of this final goal and began working to make life here on earth my "heaven." I sought satisfaction and fulfillment in earthly pursuits and tried to check off my own list of needs and wants. I fulfilled the obligations of my faith in a half-hearted manner, mostly because I knew I should and not because I wanted or cared to do so. For a while, I found myself somewhat satisfied; it was at times exciting to live according to the whims of culture and to engage in a materialistic, carpe diem way. However, it was only a matter of a few years before what seemed to be happiness began to wear off; an empty sensation lingered on the fringes and slowly crept into everything. With my faith on the periphery, my life slid into tepidity and even boredom despite having attained so much of what I thought

I wanted. At first little more than an itch, I eventually found myself haunted by a thirst for something more. I searched for fulfillment in pleasure, popularity, possessions, and whatever else I saw making others apparently happy. I was, in hindsight, half asleep. I was unable to awaken within myself that rich movement of grace that opens the eyes of the heart to the deeper realities of human existence. I was unable to understand the need to turn my heart to its true purpose, its Alpha and Omega, to the Lord of all things. This turning, conversion, I have learned, typically happens through the assistance of others who truly know the ways of Jesus Christ. In the throes of an unfulfilling existence, I needed the help of a master. I stumbled across a book by St. Francis de Sales, called *Introduction to the Devout Life*. It literally changed my life.

First, a bit on the original book will help set the stage for this present one. St. Francis de Sales published the *Introduction* in 1609 to help those he was guiding in the ways of faith embrace a more vibrant and authentic imitation of Christ, which he calls "the devout life." Devotion, as he speaks of it, "is simply true love of God."[1] As I began to pray and as I wandered through the pages of the *Introduction*, I began to remember something from my youth that I had managed to bury in all the years of wandering. I remembered, or perhaps I accepted for the first time, this truth: in Jesus Christ, God has spoken the definitive Word about our purpose. In Matthew's gospel, Jesus teaches that the greatest commandment is charity—to love God completely and to love one's neighbor as oneself (see Mt 22:37–39). To live in this way ultimately frees one from the logic of self-love and, ironically, thereby satisfies the deepest longings of the human heart. God created humanity out of love and for the sake of love. In loving, and loving correctly—not according to the demands of the world but the ways of Jesus Christ—the human heart finds its rest, true peace, and happiness.

In preparing the way for readers, de Sales focuses on the first and greatest commandment of Christ, to "love the Lord, your God, with all your heart, with all your soul, and with all your mind" (Mt 22:37). Such love requires of most people a radical reordering of priorities and relationships. From earliest times, this has been the call of Christian faith: to cast off former ways of malice and put on the new, recreated self (see Eph 4:17–24). At its heart, authentic Christian living is a life-response to the first public words of Jesus Christ: "The kingdom of God is at hand. Repent, and believe in the gospel" (Mk 1:15). The process of conversion, the faith-based journey of turning back to God, constitutes the central focus of de Sales's work.

A purification of the soul, de Sales describes conversion as, "forsaking sin and removing and cutting away whatever obstructs union with God."[2] In the early parts of his book, de Sales is quick to explain that often we will encounter a standard difficulty as we undergo conversion. When we analyze our imperfections and identify whatever else obstructs our union with God, typically a certain sadness and even frustration arises as we discover that we are not as perfect as we had previously thought. Anticipating such discouragement, de Sales notes that self-awareness opens the way to progress: "We must not be disturbed at our imperfections, since for us perfection consists in fighting against them. How can we fight against them unless we see them, or overcome them unless we face them? Our victory does not consist in being unconscious of them but in not consenting to them, and not to consent to them is to be displeased with them."[3]

In order to begin authentic living, de Sales explains, the soul must undergo a thorough purification that leads to the grace of right union with God. Living in right union with God opens the way to human perfection, and human perfection is the fulfillment for which every heart searches. With his acutely keen insight, de Sales identifies two stages of this purification. The first is the removal of sin from one's life. This happens, quite simply, by making a good Confession. While not a simple task in itself, many others have treated the topic quite sufficiently. De Sales therefore focuses more energy on a second stage of purifying the soul. Even after sin has been forgiven and wiped away, it remains attractive and the memory of sinful ways remains powerful and persuasive. This lingering affection for sin dangerously draws the soul back toward that of which it was cleansed by the grace of Reconciliation. This affection for sin is thus the focus of the second stage of purification: "Since you wish to live a devout life you must not only cease to sin but you must also purify your heart of all affection for sin. In addition to the danger of falling again, such base affections so lastingly weaken and weigh down your spirits that it will be impossible to do good works promptly, diligently, and frequently, as it is in this that the very essence of devotion consists."[4]

With that as his aim, de Sales begins the main thrust of his book by outlining the crucial undertaking of cleansing the soul of its affection for sin. To facilitate this purification, he lays out an ingenious sequence of ten thematically related meditations. He wrote them to assist the prayerful reader in understanding and correctly embracing the fullness of God's offer of life and love.

ENCOURAGEMENT FOR THE WAY

These ten meditations are immensely useful for anyone who believes in God and comes to stand before the question of life's meaning and aim. They represent, in their totality, a journey of the soul with the highest of hoped-for outcomes: right relationship with God and right understanding of one's purpose. They help to return the heart's gaze to heaven by providing immensely practical insight into what it means to live for such a noble destiny.

No doubt, these are not easy meditations to make. In addition to the challenging spiritual journey they propose, they are sometimes difficult for the modern mind and heart to engage because they were written more than four hundred years ago. They include topics the contemporary mind often considers unpopular or irrelevant, including considerations of the traditional "four last things": death, judgment, heaven, and hell. Furthermore, some of the subjects within the meditations are often dismissed as overly devotional or even outdated in the postmodern mindset: angels, demons, the saints, and the apparently flowery language of the love of God. Finally, as his word choice is particular to the sixteenth-century spiritual writers, even modern translations can be difficult to engage with centuries later.

Because of these factors, entrance into the original text often proves challenging. However, to lose the content of something so insightful and timeless would be a tragedy, principally because these meditations are among the best of ways to move from passive to active pursuit of vibrantly lived faith. The sole purpose of this present book is thus to make the contents of the original ten meditations accessible to the mind and heart of a believer many centuries after they were composed.

The following pages are simply the result of my own prayer reflections as I walked through the meditations myself, an exercise I have done now many times. They are an attempted adaptation of de Sales's ideas with a view to facilitating easier entrance into these wonderfully important subjects. The structure and order of the contents reflects the series of themes he outlines, but this book contains my own glosses and expansions upon his ideas. In effect, the whole of this work is simply a reweaving of another's masterpiece. It will thus be difficult (and I hope, unnecessary) to disentangle my thoughts from his; this meager effort is simply one more little moment in the long history of writing and rewriting the beautiful essentials of the faith, as de Sales himself noted in the preface of his own book:

> The Holy Spirit disposes and orders in many dif-
> ferent ways the devout instructions he gives us by
> the tongues and pens of his servants. Although the
> doctrine is always the same, statements of it differ
> greatly according to the various ways in which their
> books are composed. I neither can nor will, nor
> indeed should I, write in this *Introduction* anything
> but what has already been published by our prede-
> cessors on the same subject. The flowers I present
> to you, my reader, are the same; the bouquet I have
> made out of them differs from others because it has
> been fashioned in a different order and way.[5]

You hold in your hands another refashioning, and nothing
more. I simply hope to provide a new angle and approach to
something given us by one of the masters. I wrote these pages
in a place of deep prayer before the Blessed Sacrament. My aim
in putting these thoughts together is to help the next age of
believers take concrete steps toward living the timeless gift of
faith that has been so wonderfully handed on to us.

SOME PRACTICAL
POINTS BEFORE BEGINNING

Before beginning, be sure to step back and consider what you
are about to undertake. St. Francis de Sales, a Doctor of the
Church, has handed down in written form a basic roadmap
to living a more intentional and dynamic faith. In a very real

sense, you are about to take him as your spiritual guide. What a privilege!

At the outset of such a journey, a few specifics are necessary. De Sales is quite clear about the use of the meditations: the order is thematic and sequential. He suggests walking through the material one topic per day, "if possible in the morning, which is the best time for spiritual exercises," and then adds that one should "think of [the topic] during the rest of the day."[6]

The meditations are structured pedagogically, one building upon another. The first four meditations set the foundation for considering your place in God's beautiful masterwork; by design, they lay the broad groundwork for the rest of the journey. The next four meditations treat the four last things; their specific focus requires the creative application of the imagination to matters of faith. The final two meditations are briefer and more direct; they will help you make a concrete choice for the good life. Because of this intentional structure, the effect of the sequence is only truly palpable when the meditations are completed from beginning to end, in order, and without great pauses or lapses in attention. This book, then, is designed to be something of a ten-day miniretreat. Remember that some of the topics will be more difficult to engage than others but that each meditation necessarily interfaces with all of the others; they are ten topics with one goal. Prudence, good planning, and firm commitment will carry you through, so that once the meditations are begun, they can also be completed.

BEGINNING EACH MEDITATION

On method, de Sales suggests two simple steps to precede each meditation: first, place yourself in the presence of God, and then ask him to inspire you. On the first, he suggests any of four ways, each of which consists of a few moments prayerfully spent considering the reality of God's presence:[7]

- First, you might consider that God is present in all things and places.

- Second, you could consider that God is not only present in all things and places but is particularly and most significantly present in your very heart.

- Third, you may imagine Christ gazing down from the heavens to behold all people, but especially those who are at prayer and, in particular, you in this moment.

- Fourth, you might imagine Christ present to you as though he were at your side to help you make these prayers.

Choose whichever of these helps, but do not be concerned with getting this exactly right—it should be a matter of, at most, a minute of prayer. Then, proceed to the second step and ask God to inspire you. One simple method of doing so is to use the words of the prophet Samuel: "Speak, Lord, for your servant is listening" (cf. 1 Sm 3:10). Another simple and always effective prayer is, "Come, Holy Spirit." It may even be as simple as saying, "Lord, I ask you to inspire me," or something to that effect

Lift Up Your Heart

in your own words. The beginning of the day's meditation is not formalized or formulaic but rather your moment to invite the Lord to guide you. What matters most is that you begin each prayer period by giving God permission to lead the unfolding of the mystery.

ENGAGING THE MEDITATION

Having thus begun, aware of God's presence and longing for his guidance, simply read the meditation itself in a prayerful spirit. De Sales will guide you through these thematic considerations to enable you to, "return to the Lord with your whole heart" (cf. Jl 2:12). As you read, do not hesitate to pause and take some silent prayer when a particular aspect or consideration strikes you. Pause when you feel moved to do so, reread where necessary, and move at the pace that suits you.

One problem we often encounter in spiritual reading is the unintentional tendency to separate spiritual reading and prayer from the rest of life. Often, we read something beautiful, find profound insight while reading it, and then go back to doing whatever else we must do for the day. The hectic pace of a regular day occupies every ounce of our attention and we quickly forget or fail to apply the graces of our prayer and reading. To overcome such a division, de Sales makes a very practical suggestion to help us carry the contents of the meditation into the rest of our day. He calls it a "spiritual bouquet": "People who have been walking about in a beautiful garden do not like to leave without gathering in their hands four or five flowers to smell and keep for the rest of the day. In the same way, when our soul has carefully considered by meditation a certain mystery[8] we should select one, two, or three points that we liked best and that are most adapted to our improvement, think frequently about them, and smell them spiritually during the rest of the day."[9]

As you finish the meditation, make an act of gratitude for whatever good insights the Lord has given, and ask his guidance for the rest of the day. If it is helpful—and each day will be different for you—prepare a spiritual bouquet to carry forth, aside from the proposed "Focus for the day's prayer." However you choose to set out from the meditation, be sure to return frequently to the main themes throughout the day to maintain the spirit of making a "retreat-in-the-world."

A FINAL WORD OF ENCOURAGEMENT

As you begin, remember the goal: You are setting out to embrace the love of God more fully and therefore come to a greater place of peace and joy than you had previously known possible. It is the journey undertaken previously by all of the saints. Do not hesitate throughout each day to regularly call upon their assistance. In particular, Our Lady, St. Francis de Sales, and your guardian angel will be indispensable companions.

Finally, remember throughout this short journey that God is desperately in love with you. Think of that often. By his love for you he has led you to open this book. It is in love that God gazes upon you right now. Because of that love, God wants you

Lift Up Your Heart

to be supremely happy as you live your life here on earth and ultimately as you come to share everlasting life in heaven. These reflections upon the meditations of St. Francis de Sales will, I hope, carry you forward along the way. May they help you to lift up your heart and answer God's invitation to share in the blessedness of heaven for all eternity!

On Our Creation

My great and good Creator, how great is my debt
to you since you were moved to draw me out of
nothing and by your mercy make me what I am![1]

Place yourself in the presence of God.
Ask him to inspire you.

God created humanity not out of need but out of goodness
and love. God is the cause and completion of all things, the
beginning and end, point and purpose: "I am the Alpha and
the Omega, the first and the last, the beginning and the end"
(Rv 22:13). This fact exerts itself powerfully on the existence of
every created being, including yours. A sincere, honest awareness of God's real power draws us into harmony with the truth
of our being, with the meaning of our existence. Rather than
bargaining, competing, or fighting with God, embracing a deep

awareness of God's power can open us to the most effective form of collaboration in the world: cooperation with the will of God.

Throughout time, the desire to leave our mark has driven generation after generation to not only accept a prideful world-view but it has empowered the self-love that has divided human from human and humans from God since the beginning. When we really stop to look into the depths of our lives, what do we generally find at the center of our hearts? Typically, ourselves. Our many choices, plans, and goals so frequently swirl around our own desires. Knowingly or not, we enthrone ourselves, and in the tiny kingdom of our soul this enthronement gives little room for much else. We want everything just so, on our terms. Even in our marriages and families, the quintessential place of selflessness, a bit of reflection always reveals selfishness, pride, and self-service. With ourselves at the center, we work to store up riches and gain the honor of humanistic peers, rather than, in obedience to the Word, working to, "store up treasures in heaven, where neither moth nor decay destroys, nor thieves break in and steal" (Mt 6:20).

Consider this: God created us and gave us an ability to accomplish the greatest things in life: love, charity, generosity. By the nature God has given us, we are capable of eternal commu-nion with the Creator, the One who made *everything* possible in the first place, who is perfect and surpassing delight. The God of all goodness willed us gratuitously into being. Nothing impedes God's freedom, and because God created us in his image and likeness, we share in that freedom. Our freedom is so profound that we can freely choose for or against God. We can embrace or spurn the gift of real treasure, eternal life! The terrible authority given to the human person by God's gratuity is that each person is ultimately free to choose an eternity with God or an eternity without him. We gradually shape that eternal choice by the way we freely spend each and every day.

THE LACK OF PEACE TODAY

Consider the time before our existence. For ages on end, we were nothing. Only by God's goodness did we come into being. A simple prayer: "Without you, I am nothing. You are my cause, my criterion, my guide, my destiny. Oh Lord my God, thank you for life. Thank you for my life!" How rarely do we say this or something similar! How rarely do we make this humbling but simple act of thanksgiving! Were it on our lips daily, we would think much less of ourselves and much more of God and how to please him by our lives.

A spirit of entitlement quite often characterizes our present age: "I deserve this," or "I have to have that," or "If I want to do this, I will," and so on. As a result, we are quick to miss the significance of the gifts we are given and the fact that each one is a unique blessing. The fundamental gifts of God—life, faith, family, friendships, love, and so on—are the foundation of our whole existence. Unfortunately, before we even appreciate these we begin to look around, to compare and compete, rarely content with what we have, always wanting more. Rather than appreciating the blessings given to us by God, we very quickly think, "My life could be better. And here's how it could be better. And here's who has to change, what I need, and where we need to go for it to start getting better." We believe we are entitled to happiness on our own terms and at whatever cost.

Too easily, we let ourselves obsess about an unattainable horizon of perfection, an idea we create by cobbling together all the "greatest hits" of things we see in others. As we do so, we implicitly tell God (and ourselves) that what we have is simply not enough. We misunderstand the value of our present state, and in turn, we fail to see the goodness of the process by which God is leading us into the future.

THE SCULPTURE

Imagine God as a sculptor. Each person is a unique, unfinished work of art. If we admit this image, inevitably questions arise about what it would take to complete and beautify the work. We can see how easily we impose our own ideas on the process of completion. Frequently, we set about in a frantic haste to embellish, to hasten toward finality, to add our own finishing touches and to adorn ourselves as we see best. We want to be attractive to behold. We want to stand out from the crowd, to attract interest and the notice of others. We convince ourselves that this will somehow make us happy. We seek jewels and adornments, but we seek them not for the sake of beauty. We want to have, and have more, to let others know we have more, so that rather than our wishing we had better lives, they can look at us and wish their lives were better.

When we slip into this mode, we miss the fundamentals. Of much greater importance is to see the foundation—the sculpture itself—and to see it as unfinished. In prayer, we must work to recognize that a loving master sculptor has crafted each human person uniquely. By design, no two works of this sculptor are ever the same. Rather than chasing after embellishments, a better starting point lies in two related questions: "How can I best adorn the face of creation?" and "How can I best reflect the genius of the sculptor and thereby shine the splendor of God into the hearts of all those who come into my life?" Perhaps not the first questions that come to mind, but they bring us into harmony with the mind of the Almighty.

OUR ORIGIN OF GOODNESS

Our fundamental goodness does not come from ourselves, from what we do or gain. It comes from a more basic source—from who we are, from whom we came, and to whom we can freely give glory by the way we live our lives. To maintain the imagery, the sculptor knows better than the sculpture exactly how it reaches its most beautiful fullness. Left to ourselves—and this is a great and saddening mystery—we misunderstand the subtleties and unique beauties of our own lives. As a result, we tarnish or destroy them by trying to adorn ourselves according to what we think the world would like best.

The frenzied pursuit of riches and embellishments often leads us to ignore the original goodness of the sculpture itself. The race to look the best and be the most impressive has put us in opposition with one another, which leads us to division, competition, and eventually deep sadness. We are inherently unhappy with ourselves and are so often unable to believe we are beautiful, lovable, or good unless we have such-and-such and have it better than so-and-so. As we grapple with our freedom, the urgency of competition and the ticking clock of life bring us to a constant panic. Caught in the swirl, everybody is chasing happiness, few are finding it, and nobody can define it.

The pursuit of superficial embellishments and the love of riches, honor, prestige, and popularity have so caught our common eye and bewitched us as to lead us to say something we do not actually mean. Often indirectly but sometimes even directly, we tell our Creator that we are dissatisfied with the direction of the work. Often, we act as though we can and will improve upon it and do so without God's help.

As with all images, that of a sculpture breaks down. We are not simply passive artistic compositions. We are in fact completely involved in how our lives unfold, precisely because of our freedom. Therefore, we must find a balance, and therein lies marvelous and often vastly untapped potential: the sculptor wants us to be actively involved in the process of completion, and only God fully sees and understands the beauty and the complexity of each piece in its present state in view of the finished product.

Take a moment to ponder an important possibility: it could be the case that each of us is in just the right place—right here, right now, as we are. We easily miss the fact that in this place, the present moment, we can really and creatively encounter God. If God wants to encounter us here and now, he wants to take us somewhere even more beautiful. Without considering this possibility, we will always miss the joy of being in harmony with God in the present, our hands in his as he guides the process of refining and perfecting.

Worldly horizons and material dreams will always lead the creature to wrestle God's work from his loving fingers. In the race for acquisition and perfection according to the terms of the world, we chip and mar what was becoming beautiful; the haste and frenzy of comparison and competition leads to scars, gouges, and broken edges. Without the involvement of the sculptor, the original vision for the finished sculpture is never fully realized. With that comes inevitable, inherent frustration.

The solution is not as complex as we might think. In prayer, we simply acknowledge God's identity, our own identity, and our respective roles. We strive to recognize and acknowledge the real relationship we have with God. God is God, the source of being, the Creator of all things, the Divine Artist. We are the work of his hands, a creation of love meant to become constantly more wonderful because of love, through love, in love.

Whenever we forget this, we inevitably return to our tiny kingdoms, impossible to maintain. When we remember it, we unite ourselves within to the genius of God. In such union we come before the fount of true peace. God brings order and works masterful harmony as true King and Lord.

THE THREAT OF INDEPENDENCE

All of this revolves around that basic and fallen human tendency to depend too much on ourselves and to believe that too much depends on us. As we look at the course of our lives, we can easily fool ourselves into believing two separate lies. In one direction, we can convince ourselves we need no work or self-improvement; we thus fall into complacency and false confidence. In another direction, we can slip into believing we are solely responsible for all of the work of improvement; we thus become our own solo projects.

Without a humble spirit, without docility and an openness to God, we will always think too much of ourselves with regard to "finishing the project." This mindset and its many thousands of variants must die from within. If it does not, the natural tendency will be a drift away from the peace of order and harmony. God is the God of unity and beauty; the exclusion of God always brings chaos.

Whenever we choose to work alone, we make the confident proclamation, "I'm fine, I know the way." The periphery of vision is narrow, sight is short, and the virtues always flagging without the light of the One who sees all and who is Light itself.

THE START OF HEALING

It is therefore vital to admit something very important and likely very difficult. Before God, in our hearts, with a humble and perhaps embarrassed smile, we must acknowledge that left to ourselves, we so often lose the way. When we can admit that, suddenly we will notice that in the history of our rambling on the lost way, often our own faults or failings have misled us. Thus a follow-up question arises: If by our own faults and failings we so quickly get lost, and we do not like being lost, then why do we so hastily hide them? Imagine if we could turn that habit on its head and train ourselves to become quick to point out our own faults, even in laughter rather than accusation?

Ignorance and denial of our own limitations will, without fail, act like a chain on our forward progress. From the beginning, hiding our failings from ourselves and from God has never worked. Simply remember Adam and Eve, hiding, ashamed at their prideful resistance to God's plan for their good in the garden of Eden (see Gn 3).

FOCUS FOR THE DAY'S PRAYER

In quiet reflection, name your own limitations. Admit them—as many as you can recognize. Then, with a deep breath, hold them up to God's gaze and simply ask for help. Hear God say to you, "My grace is sufficient for you, for power is made perfect in weakness" (2 Cor 12:9). Then you can say with St. Paul, "If I must boast, I will boast of the things that show my weakness" (2 Cor 11:30). At first it sounds foolish. Consider this: if you were not weak, you would not need God; because you are weak, God can work in you. This means, surprisingly, that the places in your life most attractive to God are the places of greatest weakness, because in those places he can most easily undertake the work of making you whole. God sets the terms and timelines for healing and wholeness, but nothing can begin until you show the sickness to the Divine Physician.

Submit, by thanksgiving, praise, and even begging, to God. This day's task: to become humble before God. See his goodness as Creator. See how God has blessed you abundantly in giving you a nature capable of believing, of hoping, and of loving. Acknowledge, throughout this day, that without allowing God a free hand in your life, you will continue to go astray. Admit that every time you go astray you impede the perfection of his handiwork.

Only God knows every detail, and his grace and guidance will lead you to discover the way to reuniting and reordering all that falls apart. It begins with seeing his goodness and trusting in him. Pray today: "Oh God, I trust in you." God alone knows, in every tiny detail, the purpose for which he dreamed you into being: "You formed my inmost being; you knit me in my mother's womb" (Ps 139:13). He is the only one who knows how to keep undoing whatever mess you make. Only God can guide you to yourself, to your freedom, and thus to your destiny.

———

Oh my God, loving Creator, I offer myself to you, in spite of all my pride and foolishness. I do so acknowledging you as my creator, my guide, my destiny. I hold my whole life, my whole being, up to you. I surrender to you despite my constant attempts to control, reshape, and embellish. I thank you for creating me, for redeeming me, and for putting up with me. I thank you for always allowing me to throw my hands in the air and, either through tears or laughter, to see that I am small and childish. I leap into your arms, childlike, trusting you to guide me past all that I put in my own way. I love you, Lord, Father, Creator. Be with me. Amen.

On the End for Which We Were Created

My God and my Savior, you shall henceforth

be the sole object of my thoughts. . . .

You shall be the joy of my heart.[1]

Place yourself in the presence of God.
Ask him to inspire you.

A challenging thought: God does not need us. No matter how important the things we do may seem and how massive the stresses and responsibilities before us feel, God can do just fine without us. Here is a beautiful spin on that challenging thought: God could have gotten by just fine without us, but he chose not to—he chose to bring us into existence. De Sales pointedly reminds his reader, "God has placed you in this world not because he needs you in any way . . . but only to exercise his goodness in you by giving you his grace and glory."[2] By extension, this means God would prefer to do many things with and through us rather than without us. This realization is the entry point to cooperation with the plan of God.

As we have already considered, we tend to think too much of ourselves, give ourselves too much credit, and so also give ourselves too much apparent responsibility. God can do it! God can do it all. He wants us to cooperate, to collaborate, and indeed to exercise our freedom in a joy-filled submission to his good will.

A challenging question: If God doesn't need us, why are we here? Simply put, we are here because God wants to exercise his own goodness in us by giving us his grace and his glory.[3] God's infinite goodness cannot be contained, and so it overflows into creation. Creation glorifies God like a symphony glorifies its composer, as many distinct parts come together to make something far more beautiful than was ever possible had they each remained separate. Wonderfully, the human person has a significantly unique role to play in the symphony of God's creation.

Today, we admit to ourselves, "I am simply smaller, in the grand scheme of things, than I like to admit. All of my faculties, my gifts and abilities, find their meaning in knowing and loving God and loving and serving my neighbor." As source, origin, and destiny of all of creation, God draws us naturally and supernaturally toward a fullness that we could not fabricate or even imagine outside of faith and grace. In our lives, by the proper use of all of our faculties, we commune with God and encounter our purpose. By our minds we know God; by our memory we recall his goodness to us; by our will we love God; by our tongues we speak of him and sing his praises, and so on. Ultimately, our purpose is simple: to be perfectly united to God. This may not be immediately obvious or attractive to us, but it will become so with time, and in particular through the course of these prayerfully made meditations.

THE ROLE OF FAITH

A foundational question for the entire task at hand is a simple one: Where is faith in our lives, and what role does it play? Imagine a bicycle wheel with many spokes. We tend to think of balancing all of the aspects of our lives in such a way that the wheel is intact. We think of family, friends, work, rest, vacation, sleep, diet, exercise, and faith as some of the many spokes. When they are evenly distributed, the weight the wheel bears is balanced, and the wheel is effective.

Yet there is a problem with this image. We know by physics that if we remove a single spoke, or perhaps a number of evenly distributed spokes, the wheel will continue to function, at least for a while, as fewer spokes can still distribute the weight evenly. If we see faith as one spoke among many, we see it as something that we can take or leave. Certainly more spokes are better than fewer, but by this image, we operate as though faith were a removable component of the whole, a nice add-on when it works or when we find space. That which is removable is not essential, and herein lies a tremendous problem with our basic mindset.

We need to shift our paradigm from thinking of faith as a spoke on the wheel to accepting it as the center point of the wheel: the hub. In both the image and in the reality of our lives, the hub holds all of the other spokes in place and evenly distributes them. Our relationship with God is not a substitutable add-on; it is rather the centrality of our lives, the place where we encounter the deepest meaning of our existence and where our lives make contact with our eternal destiny in him. God provides the criteria by which we order and balance all the details of our lives. God is, in this way, the ultimate criterion, the lens through which we understand the life well lived.

GOD AND OUR PURPOSE IN LIFE

"I praise you, because I am wonderfully made; wonderful are your works! . . . How precious to me are your designs, O God; how vast the sum of them!" (Ps 139:14, 17). The purpose of our existence flows from God because he is intentional in the way he creates. When God is not central in our lives, when faith in God is but one of the spokes, we discover another dilemma that plagues our age: we are on our own in the quest to define the meaning of life itself. When we are not relating to God from the central place in our lives, we lose touch with our purpose and with the means of living most fully. We are stuck with the monumental task of creating our own purpose, crafting it according to our liking, and fulfilling it by our own designs.

At first, this sounds enticing, if not exciting. Unfortunately, the promise of such freedom will always disappoint. Take a walk through the self-improvement section of any bookstore: the life-purpose options are countless. Each proposes a different idea or set of ideas. When we leave it to ourselves to create our purpose, we either end up tossed about by the whims of secular society or we end up purposeless and sad. No alternative notion of purpose, insofar as it excludes authentic and total communion with God, will ever truly satisfy; none of the options out there, fabricated by generation after generation of non-believers or semi-believers, takes account of the plan of the Author of all creation and the destiny in view of which he created.

Our purpose and meaning already exist. As God says to Jeremiah so he says to us: "Before I formed you in the womb I knew you, before you were born I dedicated you" (Jer 1:5). When we do not have the contact with God that faith brings, we lose touch with that purpose; it fades into obscurity and the hazy gray of a spiritual-but-not-religious age. Then we are on our own and, as we discover over and over again, we cannot truly satisfy our deepest longings. We are not able to fulfill ourselves because we are not our own creators. Our homespun notions of purpose are always incomplete without right relation to God. St. Augustine famously sought fulfillment in the ways of the world: in possessions, people, worldly honor, and pleasure, all outside of the logic of faith. In perhaps the most profoundly important statement of Christian thought, he realized his own errors and cried out in surrender, "You have created us for yourself, oh God, and our hearts are restless until they rest in you!"[4]

We are circling the notion of being dependent on God for discovery and fulfillment of our purpose. Dependence on God often sounds like helplessness. Once more, St. Paul comes to our aid: "Therefore, I am content with weaknesses, insults, hardships, persecutions, and constraints, for the sake of Christ; for when I am weak, then I am strong" (2 Cor 12:10). Actually, dependence on God means we have the good fortune of *not* being responsible for defining happiness or creating the means to finding it. Dependence on God means inviting God to be strong in us, to guide us, to show us the way. By his providence, God has already set the way before us. Our finding it lies in the act of depending on God to show us and to lead us. We must simply let him exercise his goodness in us—which will always lead us back to him, source and destiny. How simple!

Yet how easily we get lost. We are lost as soon as we slip into thinking that we are really important, that we deserve better and are independent enough to create and know our own truths rather than submit to those revealed by God. The voice of our age resonates in our souls: "If I like it or if it feels good, it must be good, and I deserve it" and, "If I feel strongly enough about it, it must be true." Consider an example of someone who lives by these mantras. That way does not lead to joy because it excludes the guidance of the One who knows. We see it when we examine parts of our own histories or when we observe the life of someone who is in the midst of fashioning their own truth and defining their own purpose. Quite simply, life lived without God or without giving God freedom to lead oozes with the rotten fruits of frustration, anger, resentment, jealousy, and the spite of resistance. That cannot be the way, because as Jesus taught, "a good tree does not bear rotten fruit, nor does a rotten tree bear good fruit. For every tree is known by its own fruit" (Lk 6:43–44).

CHOICES, GOALS, AND DESTINY

This is about the right use of our freedom and the ability to make choices. Freedom is not ambiguous; all of our freely chosen actions have implications, choices we make in view of some goal. Take a simple and somewhat lighthearted example. If a man chooses to eat a sandwich for lunch, most likely he does so to satisfy his hunger. If he chooses in particular to eat a grilled cheese sandwich for lunch, he does so to satisfy his hunger as well as to please his taste, because in fact he prefers grilled cheese to any other sandwich. This simple choice is not isolated but related to a longer chain of goals. He satisfies his hunger— and in a pleasant fashion—in order to provide enjoyment for himself and nourishment for his body in view of performing well at work in the afternoon. He eats well in order to assist his performance because he would like a raise. He wants a raise so that he can afford a trip during the Christmas holiday for his family. He wants to take that trip because he believes it will draw his family closer together and he believes this will bring greater joy to his home. Joy in the home means richer harmony, which leads them all to thank God more heartily.

This illustration of a single chain of goals, albeit somewhat over-simplified, demonstrates a point. However distant, God *must* be the object of all our pursuits. The man does not have to claim that he eats grilled cheese solely in order to bring his family closer to God, but he can certainly acknowledge that eating the grilled cheese is, in a distant manner, related to his efforts to move toward God.

Take an alternative set of choices and goals: this same man eats the grilled cheese, but now he does so at work, in front of a group of coworkers. He chooses to do so not only to nourish his body but now primarily to impress a coworker. He knows that this particular coworker harbors a deep respect for people who eat grilled cheese. He also knows that she is recently single and is looking for a date to the company Christmas party. Here, the man chooses to eat the grilled cheese—and flaunt it—because he is subtly trying to seduce his grilled-cheese-loving colleague in hopes of extramarital romance. Where before, he could relate the grilled cheese choice to moving closer to God, now the same choice is rooted in a different final goal: his own pleasure, the pursuit of which will, if successful, ultimately destroy the harmony and health of his marriage rather than build it up.

Anything we choose to do in our lives that does not lead us in some manner more deeply into God is in fact not helpful. It either pauses or impedes our progress toward real fulfillment, toward the achievement of our purpose. The ultimate criterion of all our actions must be God. We can assess any choice or decision in light of its fitness for moving us closer to God. This does not mean we have to obsess over every grilled cheese we eat; it does mean we should be willing to ask, in small as much as great choices, "Why am I choosing this? And, if I trace that out, where is it leading me?"

However distant, if union with God is not the ultimate goal of our choices, with some introspection we discover that we have replaced God with ourselves and have begun to pursue our own wants to satiate our desire for gain and glory. St. Thomas Aquinas noted that if union with God is not our ultimate goal, some lesser good—the pursuit of riches, honor, pleasure, or power—has replaced this greatest good.[5] In our past, present, and future, whenever God is not the criterion and the goal, our activity serves some other end, some selfishness or self-service. The crux of the matter lies in realizing that any ultimate goal other than union with God will lead us to be dissatisfied, restless of heart like the young St. Augustine. A life filled with choices ordered to the pursuit of union with God resonates with the harmony of true communion, peace, and real love that satisfies the heart.

PERSPECTIVE THROUGH COMMUNION

If union with God is to become the final goal of all our efforts then, in the present moment, we have to create space for him. This requires an opening of our hearts and our lives. When we open our lives to deeper communion with God, we discover authentic self-knowledge, as we began to explore in the previous meditation. Our true identity lies in the Author of our existence who is, as we have said, also our destiny. He is our Alpha and our Omega. Between these two "moments" we *find* or discover ourselves in him who is also our guide.

Gradually, communion with God becomes more and more clearly the way we recognize the means to our real fulfillment and the achievement of our purpose. Communion with God comes about through regular prayer, reflection on the scriptures, and partaking of the sacraments. As we open up to and deepen this communion, we gradually discover a peace and joy in the present that we had not previously experienced.

As soon as this begins to happen, we start to remember the days when we did not have such peace and joy. Often, as we do so, we marvel at how easily in our past we failed to live authentic love. As we draw closer to God and see the importance of communion with him, we inevitably discover and then lament the great distance we have previously allowed to stand between us.

Vanity, pride, lust, and greed are vices that keep us, rather than God, at the center of our pursuits. Wherever we allow them space, we marginalize God. How often have these dominated our desires, our undertakings, and our energies? Truly opening our lives to God is like stepping into pure light and discovering that we have been spending all our time in a half-lit reality. The light of God reveals a lot of dirt and decay that we never used to notice. Now we see it clearly, and we realize how much it taints the goodness of the place.

KNOW THYSELF

Perhaps the greatest obstacle to choosing well in the present moment is a lack of self-knowledge. We make mistakes because we think we know what will make us happy, but we usually consult only ourselves or others without recognizing our rootedness in God our Creator. As we open ourselves to God in prayer and allow him to embrace us, our self-knowledge becomes more profound and simple. As we lower our guard and let Jesus near, we encounter him as the Way, the Truth, and the Life (see Jn 14:6). We find true freedom in him because God is perfectly free. True freedom involves knowing ourselves, knowing our destiny, and then making choices in wisdom and prudence, with insight into the mind of God.

Self-knowledge means developing a keen awareness of the past and the present, in view of a newly-hoped-for future. Part of the purpose of this meditation is to look back over our lives and see all of the ways we have chosen poorly. How much we despise in our own broken past and even this imperfect present! Keen awareness of our past sins protects us from falling backward. Only fools repeat their past, as the proverb says so sharply: "As dogs return to their vomit, so fools repeat their folly" (Prv 26:11). Grace transforms us, and self-knowledge reminds us of where we are most likely to slip again and impede God's efforts by moving backward. Praise Jesus that by his grace and by these recognitions we can make and measure progress! Praise Jesus, for with great hope we can envision a future of even greater progress past our own brokenness.

A NOTE OF CAUTION

In reflecting back over our lives, we must resist the temptation to slip into anger, self-loathing, or even despair. For the sake of self-knowledge, it is essential to reflect on the impact of sin and the rejection of God in our lives. It is just as vital to do so in view of coming to love our own histories, in particular because the stumbling lessons of the past have brought us to this very moment and to these very discoveries.

One of Christ's great lessons is that we are not to identify ourselves with our sins. Our sins are our own, certainly, but we are above them, better than them, and we can move past them. Look at the way he loved the previously sinful Mary Magdalene (see Lk 8:2) or Matthew, the greedy tax collector (see Mt 9:9). Christ tells us there is a Way for us. This Way involves faith in God and the rejection of sin: "This is the time of fulfillment. The kingdom of God is at hand. Repent, and believe in the Gospel" (Mk 1:15). Our sins—no matter how grave and many—do not define who we are. The woman caught in adultery was, by Jewish law, as good as dead. Christ said, "Neither do I condemn you. Go, and from now on do not sin any more" (Jn 8:11). For this reason, above all else, he has given us the sacrament of Reconciliation—so that we can hear, with absolute certitude, "Your sins are forgiven" (Lk 7:48, repeated in the Rite of Penance). The reality of conversion and the power of God's forgiveness should bring us constantly to our knees, but with joy at his forgiveness rather than despair at our previous failures.

Herein lies the key to embracing our past and loving God in the present: to detest those elements of our past that contain our own self-centered brokenness and selfish pursuits. We grow to abhor the sinful aspects of our own stories. Yet we do not slip into hating ourselves for who we were because the present has come out of all of that. We admit that God has shown us mercy and brought us, through the mess of our own meanderings, to this moment. Here and now, we are on track to embrace repentance and "live Jesus."[6]

This is holy self-knowledge: the graced embrace of God's mercy in our lives and the ensuing relishing of all that is good. To know our past and see our previous failings is fundamental. If our purpose is to be eternally one with God then our own historical division from him is the outline of our own greatest risks. Holy self-knowledge strengthens our resolve to ask, as we look to today and to tomorrow, "How does this—whatever it is—relate to God?" This even-keeled self-awareness with regard to our past assists us in bringing God to the center. It dislodges the fallen tendency to serve the ego that previously occupied the sin-ridden central place in our hearts. The mature consideration of our past faults is an urgent element of repentance, as it leads us to detest the evil in our own past and to cling unceasingly, joyfully, and zealously to all that leads us from it and into the bosom of a loving God.

God's love is shown, above all else, in having created us and having done so with such a noble, lofty, blessed purpose. Our purpose is to be like God—to live forever in endless joy

and perfect communion with all of the blessed. "Who am I,"
you might ask, "to deserve this?" A beloved child of God, and
one who has the freedom to live for this purpose here and now.

SHIFTING OUR HORIZONS

Still another paradigm shift awaits us. Often, we think of our
lives as a set of years unfolding before the inevitable reality of
death. We let death be the final horizon of our time and then
set about laboring to accomplish everything just right within
the set of years between now and then. Always, in this context,
the sands in the hourglass are slipping away.

Living in this way, as we usually do, the race of life becomes
an urgent one: to accomplish and accumulate quickly, so we
can enjoy whatever we have saved up before we die. We spend
decades of life chasing after more and more. Sadly, when we
are finally ready to retire and enjoy the fruits of our life's work,
we are often too old or too tired to do so. Our challenge, in
faith, is to broaden that horizon. Isaiah prophecies that God
will "destroy the veil that veils all peoples, the web that is woven
over all nations. He will destroy death forever" (Is 25:7–8). With
death as our horizon, we live trapped under the web woven
over the nations. By baptism into Christ Jesus, God has freed
us from the constraints and anxieties that rightly plague us if
we live with death as our horizon. God has changed our destiny.
Have we realized it?

Rather than death, God must be our horizon and heaven
our pursuit. This is the root of the Good News of Jesus Christ:

we do not have to die. Certainly, our souls will separate from our bodies, and this will entail pain and sadness for us and for those we love. Yet if God is our horizon and our calling is to live for eternal union with him, then eighty or ninety years is the time given us during which we are free to choose—God or self.

The core realization of this meditation is this: our earthly time is not the whole reality. It is rather the entry point into eternity. If we grasp that correctly, it changes our entire perspective. A well-lived life does not necessarily contain every material enjoyment available and every social praise and pleasure. A well-lived life leads us into eternal happiness. With death as the horizon, the urgency lies in "getting it right" here and now, prompted by our passing desires and dictated by the claims of a secular world, all before time runs out. With eternity as the horizon, and in view of the possibility of an eternity without God, the urgency lies in "getting it right" so as to move from sinful division to communion with God and one another here on earth. Only from that place of faith may we move into the eternal glory of everlasting communion with God and all of the blessed when our time on earth is complete.

THE RISK OF COMPLACENCY

A tremendous risk to our "getting it right" is complacency—to think, "Oh well, not many people are really serious about this stuff, so I don't really need to be either. I'll leave that to the fanatics." What if we could truly see, with all clarity, that our actions are not neutral, that any freely chosen action has moral value, positive or negative, good or evil? What if we finally connected these values to our eternal destiny and saw that our actions now set the course of this life, either toward or away from eternal life with God, the only life that truly satisfies? De Sales sets this as a central theme of the meditations. If we succeed in understanding horizons and the implications of our actions, we will quickly see that actions that do not ultimately lead us to God are a terrible risk. They may bring immediate pleasure, which of course is why we choose them, but in making choices like that we may be trading a passing pleasure now for an eternal one later.

As the significance of getting the horizon right crystalizes, the need to reject anything that does not lead us toward the fulfillment of our purpose becomes a primary one. A complacent spirit will lead us to put off doing good and avoiding evil. Complacency leads us to say, "I can always convert later or leave behind this or that guilty pleasure tomorrow." It leads to a lack of zeal; it encourages one to simply keep walking with everybody else and put off the real commitment for which faith calls.

The Gospel call is one for radical change right now. Jesus Christ brought so much novelty, challenge, and vigor that he caused scandal almost everywhere he went. Christianity is a religion whose founder was killed because he challenged people to get up out of their comfortable ways, their legalism or their laziness, and to start living real charity. We cannot forget this. The Gospel proclamation is a call to repentance and conversion, to "not sin anymore" (Jn 8:11). Complacency leads us to delay, subtly summarizing the Gospel call for repentance as an over-statement without any real urgency: "I'll get to that sometime, but I'm basically a good person, and for now that's enough."

A Chinese proverb tells about three demons that were brought before Satan. Satan asked them to present a new strategy for deceiving humanity. The first demon spoke up and said, "Master, we will tell them God does not exist." Satan looked at him and said, "That was once a good idea, but we have tried it for ages. It has worked, but not well enough." The second demon stepped forward slowly and said, "Rather, Master, we will tell them *we* do not exist." Satan responded, "Much better, but we have tried that as well. More effective, but not enough." The third demon then stepped forward and said, "Master, my strategy is quite simple. We will just tell them to do it tomorrow . . . whatever it is." Satan looked at them all, smiled, and said, "Go!"

FOCUS FOR THE DAY'S PRAYER

Ponder your purpose today. "Consider the unhappiness of worldly people who never think of all this but live as if they believe themselves created only to build houses, plant trees, pile up wealth, and do frivolous things."[7] God says to the man who builds a bigger barn to store all his wealth, "You fool, this night your life will be demanded of you; and the things you have prepared, to whom will they belong?" (Lk 12:20). Your purpose is far greater than you previously imagined: you are destined to share in eternal blessedness with God and all the angels and saints.

Ask yourself in prayer today, "In the practical realities of my life, where is faith?" Beg for the grace to move it to the central place in your life, rather than the margins. If that requires a significant shift, spend time freely lamenting the implications of your own sinful past and the misunderstandings that kept you from God.

Remember the things you loved and the ways you sought honor or power or wealth or pleasure. Think of the created goods with which you filled your days and your dreams in hope of satisfaction. Consider that these were all substitutes for the Supreme Good, God himself. Note the attachment to the world brought by these pursuits, the dreary chains of the constant race, the agonizing sense of never having enough, of losing time, of always wanting to be full but constantly taking more and more. Recall that almost depressing set of questions that always lingered beneath the surface of your labors: "How can I really be happy? Is it even possible? What is this deep ache with which I burn, and why will nothing quench this thirst?"

Ask further for the grace to shift your gaze from death to heaven. Union with God must become a present reality, a present choice and the object of your pursuit here and now. The eighth meditation will focus solely on heaven; for now, strive to relate your small daily choices to God and his glory rather than ego-feeding self-service. Take a deep breath and let the Holy Spirit ease your concern over your own death as you consider your real purpose. Ask the Holy Spirit to show you the joy of knowing that purpose and considering your destiny. Ask God to help you mingle that joy with a resolution to overcome apathy and complacency. With God's grace, you can finally set about, in haste like Mary when she hears of the good news of Elizabeth's pregnancy (see Lk 1:35–45), to do the good regardless of the challenges, the distance, or the risks.

"Awake, O sleeper, and arise from the dead, and Christ will give you light" (Eph 5:14). In place of complacency, ask for urgency. To live well in the present moment is to live like there might not be a tomorrow, to "stay awake, for you know neither the day nor the hour" (Mt 25:13).

Finally, give thanks. Thank God for the great gift of your life. Give thanks for a purpose as beautiful as this one. Thank God because he has bestowed upon you a unique and personal way of answering his call to love. You answer that call by the gift of his grace as it imbues your free "yes" to his action in your life. Gratitude for your noble destiny keeps you humble yet open, small yet confident, zealous and free in your efforts to "repent and believe," to imitate Christ and to ultimately share in the Good News of life everlasting.

————

Oh Lord God, I offer myself to you again and again. I offer myself, now more deeply aware of the goodness of my life and the greatness to which you call me. Please, water the seeds of this new awareness by the outpouring of your grace, and help me to vigilantly

guard against the weeds that would choke their growth
and prevent them from bearing fruit, fruit that will
last. Grant me an increase in faith, hope, and love,
that the fruitfulness of my life may be eternal! Amen.

THE THIRD MEDITATION:
On God's Benefactions

How good my God has been in my behalf!
How good indeed! Lord, how rich is
your heart in mercy and how generous
in good will! My soul, let us always recall
the many graces he has shown to us.[1]

Place yourself in the presence of God.
Ask him to inspire you.

The root of most problems, and the foundation of most sins, is pride. Through pride, we allow ourselves to be the center of our own worlds as we embrace the pervasive thought that we are greater and more independent than we really are. Pride is the principal vice that turns the soul away from real relationship with God and into the superficiality of a perfunctory faith. Why? Because faith requires an openness to God's help, God's gifts, God's love. A proud soul says, "I'm fine as I am, thank you very much. I'll reach out when (and only when) I need you." Contrary to the faith-suffocating effects of pride runs the simple, quiet, and beautiful virtue of humility. This crowning virtue opens the soul to God and to holiness as it keeps us from thinking too much or too highly of ourselves. Unfortunately, embracing humility does not tend to come easily or naturally. Fortunately, we have a very simple entry-point: gratitude. When we are grateful, we recognize that everything we have received is a gift. There is no room to think too much of oneself because gratitude helps us recognize our total dependence on the giver. In the gentle act of giving thanks, we find the soul virtuously humbled and pride uprooted.

OUR GRATITUDE LIST

Gratitude is absolutely fundamental as the attitude of a sincere son or daughter of God. Every parent knows an ungrateful child is headed for bad things. God the Father does not demand gratitude of us; rather, he shows us its value, especially through the example of his saints and holy men and women. He invites us to gratitude not because he wants our thanks but because he knows that along this way we learn to relate correctly to him and discover the way past our own sinful tendencies.

To awaken gratitude is quite simple. We need merely pause and look at our lives. No matter how rich or poor we are, or how easy or difficult a time we may have, we can always find something for which to be grateful. Perhaps one of the greatest exercises we can ever undertake as a regular part of our spiritual regimen is to make a list of all we have received.

We can always start broadly. First and foremost, we give thanks for the gift of life: as we have seen through the earlier meditations, we are blessed to be called into being gratuitously by a God who loves us. Moreover, God has given us so many supports to live our lives well. He has given us each a body, which is dignified and blessed, through which we express the sentiments and movements of the soul. He has given us health, however perfect or imperfect. He has given us life through two parents, whether we are close to or far from them. He has given us our families of origin and the families we know at present. He has given us friends, supports and aids to us in so many countless ways. He has given us so many smaller aids to enrich our day-to-day lives.

We always do well to take time and be thorough in this analysis of blessedness. We can thank God for the clothes we are presently wearing, the book we are currently reading, the chair in which we sit, and the bed in which we sleep, which most likely lies under a roof that keeps us dry and between walls that keep us warm. We can thank God for the food we have most recently eaten, for the shower we have most recently enjoyed, and even for the air we presently breathe. We ought not take any of these for granted, for plenty of people throughout the world do not have them in such blessed abundance.

So many in our world suffer from material poverty, from mental or physical disability, or from some great lack of bodily well-being. Certainly, we each uniquely share in varying degrees in these difficulties, but in so many ways God clearly has not willed it that we should suffer such trials too deeply. This thought should not lead us to a Pharisaical, "Thank God I'm not like them." Instead it must lead us to a deep appreciation of the blessedness out of which must flow our selfless charity for all of humanity: "Of those to whom much has been given, much will be expected" (Lk 12:48).

THE NATURE OF GIFTS

An important consideration, before we consider further the blessing of mental and spiritual gifts, is that of the corporeal nature of the Church. Because we are members of Christ's Body, the Church, an inherent consideration of the community must arise at this point. God has constituted the Body in such a way that it never lacks and that all of the members are in relation to one another and to him (see Rom 12 and 1 Cor 12). Whatever gifts God gives to us are not solely for our private benefit. God gives us gifts to aid us in building up his Body and bringing about the ordering of this world to the kingdom. He bestows gifts upon us in order to aid us in strengthening, empowering, healing, and blessing the other parts of the Body that are in need or lacking such gifts.

The gifts of God, the spiritual as well as the material, are for the good of the whole human family. Catholic social teaching speaks of the universal destination of goods, stating that nobody really owns anything, but all are actually stewards of the manifold gifts given them by God. Spiritual theology speaks of the corporal nature of spiritual gifts, reminding us that all gifts are given and intended to bless the whole Body of Christ, not only the recipient. These considerations help us to break out of the potential tendency to slip into pride as we take stock of our blessings.

DEEPENING THE GRATITUDE LIST

Once our basic list of gifts is complete, we can move into even more specifics. We give thanks to God for the blessings of our mental gifts. We thank God for the ability to converse and understand the spoken and written word. We give thanks for the mental capacity to reason and to reflect on these important realities. We give thanks for the education that has made it possible for us to read and ponder these very words and for our capacity to see cause and effect as we grow in devotion to God and remove the divisions that cause sadness. We can give thanks for the timing of our existence, for the gift of living in a time and place where we are free to reason, converse, and engage these matters. We can give thanks for the upbringing and life relationships through which we are at present less ignorant of his goodness than we once were and, but for his grace, might still be today.

Many people are born with mental deficiencies or difficulties greater than our own. None of us is perfect, but we can always discover a place in our own mental capacities where we are blessed. Perhaps we could have been born with a psychological disability or without the ability to speak or interact with others or relate to the world around us. We were not—and for this, we must give thanks. Again, this thanksgiving is not in view of building up a prideful disdain for those who have less but rather to empower us to see that we are blessed not accidentally but for a task, and that task is the building up of the Body of Christ. Wherever and whenever these exercises of gratitude lead us to compare ourselves to others in ways that lead to judgment or superiority, we have strayed from the good that God wills. These exercises are always for the sake of humbling us and opening our souls to God, nothing less and nothing more.

Finally, a thorough consideration of our spiritual blessings brings our gratitude list to its fullness. In creating us as we are, God has blessed us with such a beautiful calling and destiny, our nature and purpose upon which we focused during the previous meditation. For this alone every human person has cause for rejoicing. That destiny, we know, is lived through the practice of faith and our ever-deepening relationship with God. We can and must give thanks for the gift of faith. No matter where we grew up or how we learned about our faith, the fact that we are reading these very words and considering these very truths is a testament to the gift of faith that God has given to us.

At this moment, we can also consider ourselves blessed to know God through the gift of his Church. God gave humanity a Church, that faith could be known and lived throughout every age and against every opposition—even the full opposition of evil, as Christ said to Peter, "You are Peter, and upon this rock

I will build my Church, and the gates of the netherworld shall not prevail against it" (Mt 16:18). Certainly this age provides many alternatives to religion and to Catholicism. We can give thanks for the gift God is presently bestowing on us through these meditations, richly rooted in the tradition of the Church. We can give thanks that despite all obstacles, internal and external, we are open to God's work through the Church, which we know to be the sacrament of salvation.

SACRAMENTAL AND SPIRITUAL BLESSINGS

In a perfect corollary to the considerations of the last meditation, we must also look back over our lives and recognize the abundant blessings of the sacraments. Every sacrament is a means of God's blessing us with grace, of God's pouring forth his assistance that we may adhere more and more each day to the truth of the Gospel. In every sacrament, God has touched our souls and changed them for the better. We ought to consider with great attention each and every sacramental moment of our lives. While we cannot remember our Baptism if it occurred in infancy, we truly give thanks for that sacrament which has made all of the others possible. We owe it to ourselves to study the rich effects of that sacrament and thus discover the tremendous gift we have received.

We ought to meditate on our First Communion, even if we do not remember the details. We give thanks to God for the

circumstances of our lives that made that great day possible—
giving thanks for our parents or guardians who gave us our
Catholic education and the formation that made that reception
possible. We give thanks for the Church in which we received
it, for the people with whom we made our First Communion,
and for the priest and servers and ministers and everyone else
present that day who helped make it possible. Indeed, although
it might seem a bit excessive, we might give thanks for each and
every single Mass we have since attended. In gratitude, often
very little is worth overlooking!

We can recall in gratitude the special anointing that was
our Confirmation, when our baptismal graces were brought
to completion and a special outpouring of the Holy Spirit was
given to us for living the Gospel as missionaries—even if we do
not yet feel we have responded to that grace.

Whatever our state in life—married, ordained, consecrated,
religious, or called to generous single life—we can daily give
thanks for the blessing of such particular vocations and the
sacramental graces that enrich these commitments. If we have
not yet discovered the particular vocational path by which God
calls us to himself, we give thanks for the fact that it exists and
that, in his time, God will draw us to its discovery.

Of utmost importance in these spiritual considerations is
gratitude with regard to forgiveness, and especially regarding
the sacrament of Reconciliation. In our previous meditation,
we sought to truly delve into our own sinful past and know and
accept ourselves as sinners. However, that exercise alone can

tend to feel somewhat gloomy when undertaken in isolation. It must constantly be balanced with gratitude for forgiveness. Notice how clearly we remember the sins of our past! Once again, this memory can be an aid against falling back into old habits. However, notice how easily one can give these memories too much power and how quickly they can mire the soul in guilt and regret. We must remember that because of Christ's great sacrifice and because of the sacramental graces we have received through his Church, these sins are gone! Only the human guilt and memory remain: "As far as the east is from the west, so far has he removed our sins from us" (Ps 103:12).

If we remember the sins so easily, why do we not remember just as readily and freely each and every single reconciliation? Why do we let the devil accuse us so often of being wretched and worthless because of our past faults and fail to recall the *spiritual miracles* that have destroyed the effects of these sins? Every reconciliation is an encounter with the mercy of God and a restoration of the vital principle within us, charity itself. We do well to think back over these sacramental gifts. We do well, too, to spend time with the prodigal son (see Lk 15:11–32) and thank God for his fatherly embrace.

Beyond the sacraments, what about every other spiritual gift God has given us? Each of the baptized is endowed with particular gifts and abilities: "And he gave some as apostles, others as prophets, others as evangelists, others as pastors and teachers, to equip the holy ones for the work of ministry, for building up the body of Christ, until we all attain to the unity of faith and knowledge of the Son of God" (Eph 4:11–13). God has also given all of the baptized unique spiritual abilities called *charisms*. Many times we have not fully unlocked these charisms, but we can be assured that they are present. Each of us has received a particular set of spiritual gifts through the sacraments, gifts designed by God to aid us in all of the particular circumstances of our lives in pursuit of holiness. We give thanks for even those gifts we do not yet see but know by faith he has given.

We can also give thanks for each and every inspiration, aspiration, and spiritual insight we can remember. It might be as simple as remembering a moment in your childhood when you asked a question of your parents about Jesus and you still remember the answer. It might be as complex as discovering, in the tapestry of our own personal histories, the clarity that comes in looking back and recognizing the powerful ways God's providence has been at work to bring us to this present moment.

This is but a sampling of the type of "gratitude list" we can devise. This exercise is absolutely essential to our spiritual growth and to our maintenance of humility against the temptations of pride and self-centeredness. We ought to undertake this exercise often, and to conclude it by holding up all of our gifts before the Father's gaze. As we do, we should beg for the grace to always be worthy stewards and joyful recipients of his superabundance.

STEPPING BACK IN GRATITUDE

The exercise of stirring up gratitude cannot but stir up marvel at the goodness of God. When we consider the blessings of our lives, we allow ourselves to connect these blessings to a God who is all good, all loving, and always at work to bring about our fullness. The marvels he has worked in our lives are incredible! His tender care and involvement in so many details, the depths of his mercy, the constancy of his blessings and the power of his grace, all stir a recognition both of his Almighty stature and of his incredibly intimate involvement in our personal stories. It should cripple the mind and the soul, in a certain way, to think that we are only able to perceive a minuscule fraction of the whole. God is at work in our lives in countless ways we may never see. Much more broadly, God is at work in this way in literally billions of lives throughout the entire world, even at this very second. The omnipotence and omnipresence of God is stunning. It should make us feel spoiled, really, that he is so gentle and present as to be involved in our details.

Now we can pick up a practice from our last meditation. The awareness of past faults protects us from returning to them. Here as well, the consideration of past ingratitude strengthens us against failing to be grateful in the future. As we step back in gratitude and marvel at the abundance of God in our lives, we certainly are right to feel a certain sadness at our past ingratitude. How often in the past have we been like little children before the Christmas tree, tearing through the presents and setting them haughtily aside whenever they are not exactly what we want? How often have we made demands of God and then complained to him when his answer is not exactly according to our terms and expectations? How many times have we been like spoiled children and pushed away his gifts—"not this one, not like that, not now, not here"—and on and on?

Again, we have to be well aware of our past stumbling in this area so we do not risk repeating such error. How many times have we received his gifts on our own terms and bent them to our own selfish purposes? Sometimes God denies our requests because we do not understand what we are asking. Other times he denies us because he knows the harm we will bring through this or that gift. Finally, he often refuses to answer us because we ask for the wrong things at the wrong time. A hammer is an instrument for building up, for construction, but put in the hands of a child who does not understand how to use it—regardless of whether or not the child asked for it—a hammer can be quite destructive!

The difference in these matters is always between being childish and being childlike. The task is to move from one to the other, progressing in simplicity. God gives us many blessings. Many times the blessings are not exactly as we would have liked or when we would have liked. Our meditations on God's goodness and his power to be at work throughout his creation must stir us to see that he knows exactly what he gives and what he takes away and why. God is not haphazard in his workings, and we must learn to embrace that fact in total trust.

Mother Teresa used to say, "Take whatever He gives and give whatever He takes with a big smile."[2] The trust of a little child is so important, in particular because we cannot love one whom we do not first trust. Whatever we receive from God, we should always ask how we can best put it to use for his glory, because he gives it to us for a reason. We must always hear Paul's words to the Ephesians: "In him we were also chosen, destined in accord with the purpose of the One who accomplishes all things according to the intention of his will, so that we might exist for the praise of his glory" (1:11–12).

FOCUS FOR THE DAY'S PRAYER

Lift up your heart to God, recalling that invitation from the center of the Mass, the Church's greatest prayer. Hold your heart up before God, now more than ever aware of your own past, marked by sinfulness and ingratitude. Hold up your heart before God to ask his strength and blessing. As your self-knowledge deepens and your distaste for sin grows, beg his mercy and love to enrich your longing for real, lasting communion.

Spend time today making a list of all that God has given you. Love of the gifts will lead you to love the Giver; truly, gratitude is a means to loving God more fully. Through this exercise, pray for a deepening of the spirit of gratitude. Through gratitude, ask for the grace to overcome what is childish in you and the help to become more childlike, rejoicing in gifts and blessings. Firmly resolve always to cherish what God gives you. Ask God for the grace to ask, out of that gratitude, how you can apply yourself and your gifts more fully to the building up of the Body of Christ, to bringing about the kingdom, and striving for the gift of eternal life.

Principal among your good resolutions must be an ever-greater commitment and recourse to prayer and the sacraments; ask God to help you engage ever more fully the rich life of grace to which God calls you through his Church. Through these graces, God can make of you whatever he needs and bring you to be exactly as he planned.

––––––––

Jesus, thank you. I beg you to open my eyes to the amazing abundance you have bestowed upon me. Grant me fresh insight into your tender, constant care. Show me, in all of the details, all you have done to protect me, bless me, and strengthen me so that I may arrive at this very moment with a heart like this. Please, let me never take one glance, one grace, or one gift for granted. Open and widen my heart, so that in gratitude, I may always see the path ahead of me, in you. Jesus, thank you. Amen.

THE FOURTH MEDITATION:

On Sin

No, Lord, nevermore, with the help of your
grace, no, nevermore will I abandon myself
to sin. Alas, I have loved it too much. I
detest it and I embrace you, the Father of
mercy. In you I wish to live and die.[1]

Place yourself in the presence of God.
Ask him to inspire you.

Having meditated upon creation, having considered the purpose given to humankind by God, and having prayed over the blessings that God has given, the next topic for prayer is sin. By way of reminder, de Sales's aim is to facilitate the removal of our affection for sin. When he speaks of those persons who have not purified themselves of their affection for sin, he says they, "begrudge giving them up, talk about them," and would partake of them if they could. He says that they delight in staying close to them and are jealous of those who continue to linger in those sins.[2] They are like the gambler who has sworn off the habit but continues to wander through the casino; deep in his heart, he hopes to fall again. De Sales uses another image, that of, "a woman who detests her illicit love affairs but still likes to be courted and pursued."[3] Beyond the constant risk of sinning again and in the same ways, "such base affections so lastingly weaken and weigh down your spirits that it will be impossible to do good works promptly, diligently, and frequently."[4]

Again, de Sales sets out these meditations because "by the help of God's grace they will be very helpful in rooting out of your heart both sin and the chief affections for it."[5] Although we have already looked at sin and have sought to deepen our own distaste for it and to thereby reject it, de Sales now asks us to spend an entire meditation on the very topic to more fully understand what we reject and what we must let die.

THE CLEANSING OF THE FALSE SELF

From a very young age, we are trained to set goals and accomplish them on our own, by the sweat of our brow (perhaps ironically, that's a reference to Genesis 3:19). A spirit of ambition and accomplishment tells us to compete and stay strong. We find ourselves forced to build up a sense of confidence that leads us to project a strong self-image to the world around us. We look ourselves in the mirror and say, "You can do it. Nothing can stop you. Be strong." With time, we hide our limitations for fear of appearing weak in asking for help or showing our soft spots. Over the years, we build up layer upon layer of false confidence to construct the image of ourselves that we project to the world. We build our confidence not on who we are at our core but on who we want to be or think the world wants us to be. Herein lies a principal cause of what we have already called lacking self-knowledge.

Because of this process, over time we lose touch with our true selves. If a vocation is a specific call to make a total gift of ourselves then this lacking self-knowledge is tragically harmful to vocational fulfillment. How can we, how dare we, give what we do not know? Imagine giving a gift to someone you claim to love without knowing what is inside. In order to make true progress—not in terms of worldly success but in terms of becoming more and more ourselves and in terms of deepening communion with our eternal loving Father—we have to strip away the false layers and really get to know ourselves. We must tear down whatever walls we have built up, walls designed to hide our true selves from the world. We must truly be ourselves before God and then before others; if we cannot be so, we cannot give of ourselves, to God and to others. If we cannot enter into our own personally lived gift of self in imitation of Christ's self-gift on the Cross, we will never truly find the fulfillment God longs for us to know.

Certainly, all of this requires the virtue of humility acquired by a spirit of gratitude, as we have already considered. But it also requires a more detailed look at sin and the lies we have either

woven or accepted about ourselves, about others, and about
life itself. Then, and only then, can we allow God to reestablish
us in grace, with hearts set on eternity. Getting there involves a
reorienting and a reordering of what has fallen into disrepair,
neglect, or disorder.

Recall in Matthew's gospel as Christ entered into his Father's
house, the Temple, he found the money changer tables, emblems
of greed, idolatry, and selfishness, set up throughout the entry
space. He drove out the merchants, turning over their tables
and creating chaos. He did so in order to reclaim the house and
re-establish it as a worthy dwelling. In the New Covenant, the
Temple is the heart of the believer. In prayer, on the threshold
of deeper conversion, the believer must call Christ into his or
her soul and allow him to restore that worthy dwelling, to turn
over the tables of pride, greed, profit, and idolatry that fill the
space just as they filled the entryway of the Temple at Jerusalem. Christ's work, both in the gospels and in the human heart
of the new covenant, is to cast out all that does not belong in
such a worthy dwelling so that God's place can be firmly (re)
established. For this reason the meditations turn, once again
and now more deeply, to the subject of sin.

This meditation consists of three principal movements.
First, an examination of sin and the conscience. Then, a deep
and sincere repentance for that sin. Finally, a commitment to
be vigilant in uprooting and opposing sin.

THE NATURE OF SIN

The first movement in prayer is to consider sin itself. Sin is a freely chosen act that isolates us from God and inflicts harm on ourselves and our relationships. Remember Genesis: God placed Adam and Eve in the garden and showed them his whole beautiful plan of creation. He made a single rule: "You are free to eat from any of the trees of the garden except the tree of knowledge of good and evil. From that tree you shall not eat" (Gn 2:16–17). Adam and Eve looked at the entire plan of God, understanding his will, and effectively said, "Thank you God, but we're going to go ahead and do what we want to do rather than what you want us to do. We choose our desires over your will." Sin is the choice, whether by curiosity, pride, or any other vicious tendency, to pursue what we want when that differs from what God has revealed to us as good.

From the same Genesis passages, we discover sin's effects. After the first sin, Adam and Eve quickly covered their nakedness and hid from God. Sin introduced division. It divided man and woman, and as it broke their original harmony, it led them to hide their bodies from each other. What is more, it divided them from God; they quickly hid themselves from him among the trees of the garden out of shame. When God asked what happened, neither took the blame. The man said the woman gave him the apple, and the woman blamed the serpent for tempting her. Thus, in addition to bringing division, sin brings strife and accusation.

Now consider a further effect of sin. Philosophically, God is the source of all good. In him there can be no evil, no imperfection, no sadness, no failing. Union with God thus brings true peace and joy. If sin is a division, a choice against God and a separation from him, then it is a separation from the source of all goodness and joy. In simple terms, if sin separates us from God, sin makes us unhappy. This fundamentally important point will help us understand the ultimate threat sin poses to our eternal blessing.

BACK TO THE BEGINNING
. . . AND EVER SINCE

How long has it been since we first sinned? As soon as we were old enough to know the difference between right and wrong, we were able to sin. Those first sins were usually quite simple, and the guilt came quickly. Over time, the conscience has numbed and the sins have become many. What would have once caused an ache of the soul in sadness is often little more than a pinprick to the conscience. Imbued with a spirit of complacency, the soul grows comfortable or even lazy in the presence of sin and the conscience becomes numb. Sin has a way of seeping into the corners of our lives and making itself quite at home in the soul.

So often, when we encounter someone who has lived a life of obvious sin, we discover they are unrepentant and without remorse. Often, they no longer even see the sin as sin. When someone spends enough time divided from God they get used to the darkness; the soul adjusts to the gloom like the eye to dimmed light. The picture of Saul on the road to Damascus in Acts 9 is fitting: the light of God literally blinds him because he had become so accustomed to the darkness of living in opposition to God. Over time, sin mires the heart and chains it to earthly pursuits until it no longer recalls the sweetness of the movement toward God for which it was created.

Usually, as we approach a serious consideration of our own sinfulness, we give ourselves the benefit of the doubt. We say to ourselves, "Well, I'm not *that* bad. . . . I've never killed anyone or anything like that." We fail to see that all sin leads toward the suffocation of God's life in us, for "the wages of sin is death" (Rom 6:23). In considering our own sinfulness, we must remember several important facts. Grave sins are called "mortal" because, by choosing to give them place in our lives, they inflict a deadly wound upon our souls, one that, if not brought to Reconciliation, is significant enough to place our eternity at risk. In the gradation of gravity, smaller sins usually give way to greater like dirt gives way to infection. Furthermore, sins are not limited to external action; there are also inner movements such as sinful desires and sinful thoughts. Finally, it is important to remember always that sin is not just what we do but also what we do not do; there are sins of commission as well as sins of omission, intentionally failing to do the good we ought to do. All sin, great or small, leads us away from the, "glorious freedom of the children of God" (Rom 8:21), for as Jesus taught, "Amen, amen, I say to you, everyone who commits sin is a slave of sin" (Jn 8:34).

All of this sets the groundwork for a deep examination today, in hope of rooting out the causes of brokenness of our lives. A good examination of conscience is like initiating a deep cleanse. As porous skin fills with oil and dirt, so the soul becomes layered in grime. A superficial cleansing may enhance the appearance initially, but generally a more detailed inspection of each and every corner reveals that the stickier stuff has really settled in. Through prayer, grace, and sacrament, the soul is freed from sin and experiences that glorious freedom known only in God.

THE BEGINNINGS OF AN
EXAMINATION OF CONSCIENCE

The second movement of this meditation is to become aware of and then renounce your sin. As a starting point, call upon God's grace and ask for his insight. God will assist you in being honest and thorough, and his light will shine on all the dark places that need particular attention. Before moving into considering particular sins, ask more generally about your own sinful inclinations; ask yourself what tendencies generally lead you to choose to do wrong. For example, are you generally a proud person? Are you generally unhappy with what you have and so look at others' lives with jealousy? Do you delight in hurting the reputations of others? Do you place too much value on appearances and impressions? How do you value possessions? How do you approach members of the opposite sex? While all of these often point to particular sins, questions like these help to draw out the broader movements or inclination to sinfulness and in turn provide starting points to opposing sin's return.

Once we spend some time reflecting honestly and in humility on these matters, the depth and breadth of our sins quickly becomes apparent. Here, again, is an element of the process of deepening self-awareness. Beginning this process of rooting out particular habitual sin affects each person in a different way. For some it is easy, even a relief. It comes quickly and without much stress or reorienting.

However, for others it can be jarring and disappointing, especially if a person has lived with a lot of fabricated or false confidence for a long time. Often, when someone first undertakes a sincere examination and asks the Lord in all seriousness to humble them, they slip into what seems like a tailspin. The process of moving from false reality to truth causes a sense of vertigo; people often say, "I don't know who I am anymore," or "What's wrong with me? I used to be so confident and in control, and now I'm a mess!" While initially disorienting, this is actually part of the spiritual process of reorienting and reprioritizing one's whole life.

Dramatic as it was, St. Paul's conversion serves as an image and an archetype for the rest of humanity. His old life literally made no sense once he truly encountered the love and the mercy of God. At first shocking and painful, a certain interior death had to occur that would lead to new life. He says, "But now you must put them all away: anger, fury, malice, slander, and obscene language out of your mouths. Stop lying to one another, since you have taken off the old self with its practices and have put on the new self, which is being renewed, for knowledge, in the image of its creator" (Col 3:8–10). Conversion is something of a death but all in view of truly living.

THEMATIC INGRATITUDE

To lean back upon the last meditation, underpinning many of our discoveries as we examine our consciences is the theme of ingratitude. As we develop a deeper awareness of God's generosity, we can see with increased clarity how much he has done and how much he has given us throughout our lives. Each sin is in some way a choice to reject or misuse God's gifts. Were we more grateful, we would not be so hasty to spurn them, knowing they come from goodness and are given for goodness. De Sales says the sin of ingratitude "reaches out to all the rest and makes them infinitely more enormous."[6] Try to think of all those moments just before a sin—remember that twinge of conscience, the little tiny voice within that said, "Should I really do this?" Think of all the times you gave something a second thought, hesitated momentarily, and then decided to do it anyway knowing it was wrong. Think of all the warnings or even chastisements of those who love you—your parents, your teachers, your friends and neighbors, whomever. How right they were! Consider all of the times you acted quickly to avoid having to think too much about the consequences or the morality of the action. Remember feeling terrible afterward, empty and guilty. Then remember that as soon as the feelings faded you returned quickly to the sin. The list goes on—but you can consider each of these as moments when the Lord sought to intervene, either directly or by stirring the conscience. Each of these interventions was an attempted gift. Had a spirit of gratitude run deeper, perhaps you would have seen the gift God held out in seeking to intervene and thus save you from the sadness, the weight and guilt of sin.

GIFT IN SACRAMENT

Among all of the gifts that God gives us to help us avoid sin, the sacraments stand in a particular place, given to strengthen our pursuit of heaven. How many times have you been unfaithful to what you received through the sacraments of Initiation? Baptism incorporated you into the Body of Christ and forgave sin, and Confirmation strengthened and completed those graces. Yet each time you have sinned gravely, you chose to break that communion by rejecting your own identity and spurning the graces meant to keep you incorporated and in communion. If you are married, consecrated, or ordained, what infidelities have you allowed that destroy your promised communion with your beloved? Fidelity in the future is rooted in despising its absence in the past.

What of the great sacraments of the Eucharist and Reconciliation? Have you always approached them reverently, with an open and contrite heart, aware of the enormity of the gift God makes of himself and of his mercy to you? These are tremendous gifts meant to build upon the graces of the other sacraments you have received and to strengthen you broadly in your life.

Have you really let God go to work in your life through these two overwhelming blessings? Or have you let yourself fall into routine, distraction, and the droning fulfillment of obligation?

Remember also that the sacraments are not magic tricks; they do not miraculously change us into who we know we should be. The sacraments are God's gifts given to a totally free human person. Without the right understanding and disposition, we squander the grace and limit its effects. To truly understand the sacraments takes prayer and study. With due attention, we discover the sacraments are the greatest gifts God has given us because they are fundamentally indispensable aids to our salvation. God gives them to us through the Church to assist us in fulfilling our purpose in life. To either avoid them or receive them ungratefully or unworthily is a tremendous act of ingratitude. The faithful have a right to the sacraments, but God has a right to expect of us that we receive them with open, prepared, attentive, and humbled hearts.

You can ask, in looking back over all of this, what fruit the sacraments have borne in your life. Have you allowed the graces of your Baptism and Confirmation to keep you deeply intertwined and in tune with the life of God in you and in his Church? Have you allowed the Eucharist to nourish your love of God, strengthen your soul, and aid you in carrying forth from worship the charity of Christ into the world? Have you allowed Reconciliation to purify your soul and strengthen your resolve to avoid sin? If you are married, have you let the graces of Holy Matrimony constantly intertwine two hearts into one in fidelity to the covenant forged in, through, and by God? If ordained or consecrated, have you let the graces of sacrament, promise, and vow strengthen your prayer, your chastity, your obedience, and your pursuit of simplicity?

Wherever your answers to these questions are not resounding with positives, you will find failures in gratitude and, in turn, failures to respond freely to the most important gifts God gives. This list is both a starting point and an indication of the type and depth of questions with which to challenge yourself. While a good examination may be tiresome and time consuming, as a crucial part of the journey to living like Christ this regular exercise prepares you to come before him, to see the weight of your own failings, and to repent and despise them.

TO CALVARY

Recalling the contents of the previous meditations, now allow yourself to enter for a few moments into misery. Let your prayer take you to the foot of the Cross to ponder the weight of your sins. The purpose of this period of prayer is not to inflict self-hatred or ceaseless despair but to engender remorse, repentance, and reform. Carrying the list of sins you have considered, now take a moment to pause, call once more upon the Holy Spirit, and go to Calvary.

Within the temple of your soul, climb Mt. Calvary. In prayer, walk through the Passion of Christ. Take time with the gospel accounts of his suffering and death. Beg the Lord to show you that these sufferings of his were not generic but personal and that he underwent the agony of the Cross for you. Carrying your sins, bring yourself to stand at the foot of the Cross and see the lashes and lacerations of his body. As you look on, let yourself see that these are the fruits of your own sins, your own rejection of Jesus Christ. What is the Cross but humanity's rejection of God? By sin, you reject God. Resolve to never look at the Cross without seeing it as a real possibility of human freedom . . . you are so free as to utterly reject God, and by such rejection inflict terrible wounds.

As you stand before his Cross, imagine Christ looking down at you, peering into your soul, instructing you and pleading with you by his silent gaze. Do not look away; hold his gaze, and let him tell you with his tears and his precious blood how much the sin of humanity agonizes him.

If your prayer leads you further, go to him and console him as he hangs crucified. Place your hands in his hands, letting the heads of the nails press against your palms. Note that even the slightest touch of the nails would cause you to recoil. Do not flee. Let Christ hold you there, in your prayer, so that no matter how busy you become or how far you stray, you can never forget the power of his sacrifice. For you. Embrace him as he hangs on the Cross. Allow him to tell you, heart to heart, what he told Mother Teresa: "You did it to me." Let him tell you that he submitted to it all . . . because he loves you and he wants to save you from your sins.

Still upon Calvary, now place yourself at the foot of the Cross and kneel with the whole, heavy awareness of your sins. Humble yourself, with the sinful woman in Luke's gospel,[7] to reverence the feet of the Lord. Before the Cross, step forward and kiss the blood-soaked feet of your crucified Lord. In prayer, beg his forgiveness. Remember, as you stand at Calvary, it is by his precious blood you are redeemed—"the Blood of the new and eternal Covenant," as the Mass says, the blood of the Lamb of God. The whole of your purpose and destiny is possible because he has entered the great sanctuary of heaven by this sacrifice, and he has called you to follow after him. Before you can do so, you must become small, childlike, and humble.

As you behold the wounds of the Savior in sorrow, let the weight of your sin press upon you. Know that you kneel with Peter in the boat—"Go away from me Lord, for I am a sinful man!" (Lk 5:8). Know too that you are just like the prodigal son, having squandered the gifts given you by the Father. Know that you are like the adulterous woman in John 8, guilty . . . but loved past your sins. Above all else, wherever your prayer takes you, stand back up and place yourself between John and Mary, who stood there on Calvary until the last moment. Let them hold you up as the weight of the whole scene crushes down on your soul; find solace in their embrace. At the foot of the Cross, you can finally leave behind all fascinations and dark fixations with the ways of the world and recognize the truth of what is at stake: everything. All is possible . . . because he loves you so.

———————

As you step back from that place and return to your examination, once again beg God for assistance. Ask over and over for the grace to see how destructive sin can be, and beg for the grace to avoid it at all costs. Renounce your sinful past. When you are comfortable, make a formal departure from your "old self" in what de Sales calls a General Confession. In this holy and prayerful act of sacramentally renouncing former ways, you confess not in type and number but in broad strokes all of the sinful movements of your entire life. The resolution is simple: to live a better life, to avoid sin and whatever leads you to it, and to be ever more open to God's grace and mercy.

THE GARDEN OF THE SOUL

The third movement of this meditation is to set in place firm resolutions to oppose sin in the future. For this, a simple but helpful image for the soul is that of the garden. A garden is meant to be beautiful and fruitful, filled with life and fragrance, but a garden must be maintained. If a garden has been untended for many years, it will require much attention to restore its beauty and vitality. A cursory pass through the garden will immediately reveal many things growing there that do not belong. An untended garden appears obviously overgrown and disordered, and a single sweep, a quick examination, will never be enough. To restore a garden to its full fruitfulness often requires long hours and sometimes even years of careful work, focused planning, and constant vigilance. Regardless of all of that, at a certain point you must make the choice to reclaim and restore the garden. At that point, quite intentionally, you may sit down right in the middle of the garden and carefully inspect all of the life that is there, as we are here striving to do.

What plants are fruit bearing and will bear good fruit? What plants threaten the good ones and therefore threaten the harmony of the whole garden? More important, what are the weeds? These are the sins. For the present meditation, a cursory or hurried listing of types of sins and degrees of threat is not enough. Careful consideration facilitates an intentional and exhaustive identification of the weeds that, in turn, enables you to uproot them and vigilantly guard against their future return.

As with most weeds, so with most sins that have had a place in our lives for a long time: if we are hasty in our work of uprooting them, they will grow back quickly. When one sets out to weed a garden in haste, one generally pulls at the leaves of the bad growth and removes whatever is visible above ground. Having done so, it appears the weed is gone, and then, only days later, it returns. Weeds often spend a long time growing beneath the surface before they break the soil to grow strong and choke the rest of the garden. For this reason, a regular turning over of the soil is important, via examinations of conscience and sacramental forgiveness. For this same reason, a careful uprooting of each weed means identifying its type and digging far beneath the surface to pull not just the leaves but the whole root system. Sins such as lust, gluttony, greed, anger, and quick judgment often have deep root systems and affect many facets of our lives and many layers of our relationships. We may quite quickly stop looking at others with lust, stop gambling or yelling or saying harmful things, but to root out the sins themselves, we must strive to undo whatever allows them to take root in the first instant—the glance, the tinge of a greedy thought, the persistently judgmental conversations we allow, the choice to stew over an argument or hold a grudge, and so on. If we do not learn the roots of the sins that have a way of dwelling in the garden, we will not be able to vigilantly oppose them.

Each of us must make our own personal journey into the garden to remove the weeds. Contrition arises from a heart that sees the agony sin causes, from a soul that recognizes broken communion is deadly, and from a person who realizes by grace that he or she is called to love. Dethroning the self, trusting the Master Craftsman, admitting that we often make mistakes, and living gratitude are all essential.

In all of this, we pray for an increase in faith. By faith, we are able to see Christ's image in others and so avoid using them, objectifying them, dismissing them, harming them, or hating them. By compassion, we are able to see others as Christ does: as sinners who are greatly in need. What once annoyed us about others now stirs us to love and compassion, for we see them just as we see ourselves: broken and wounded. Everyone suffers weakness and sin. Grace helps us to see and be aware of that human reality. Rather than seeing life as a race to be better than everyone else, we try by faith to see it as a journey, a pilgrimage we all make together. In charity, we can strive for the true friendship of Christ by which he assists us in seeking the good of the other, whoever the other may be. In gratitude, we will never take for granted all we have been given, and we will never hoard it for ourselves.

FOCUS FOR THE DAY'S PRAYER

Today, take notice all of the small places of sin in your life. Watch carefully for its approach; notice all of the opportunities each encounter and each occasion presents. For the remainder of the day, repeat the movements of this meditation: prayerfully consider sin and its effects. Watch for it. Repent of it. Before the Cross, renounce it in your life. Finally, firmly resolve to avoid it, with vigilance, to allow the garden of your soul to flourish and bear good fruit.

Oh God, patient and loving Father, you have stood
by me in great love throughout my life, waiting for
me to recognize my failings. You have waited until
this very moment to draw me beyond my own child-
ish limitations and help me to come to full stature

according to your original plan. Lord, I remain sinful, but I beg you now to increase my distaste for all that divides me from you and from my brothers and sisters. I kiss the wounds of Christ with greater love than ever, and I desire nothing more than to be free of the wounds that keep my own heart from fullness.

I entrust my heart to you anew, forever and with great zeal. Dwell there, Lord God. By your presence and by your sacramental grace, cast out all that does not belong. Lord God, I need you, I love you, I cherish you. Thank you, thank you, thank you! Amen.

THE FIFTH MEDITATION:
On Death

O world, since I do not know the hour
when I must leave you, I will no longer
set my heart on you. My dear friends, I
will no longer love you except with a holy
friendship that can last eternally. Why should
I unite myself to you in such wise as to be
forced to give up and break our union?[1]

Place yourself in the presence of God.
Ask him to inspire you.

In Rome, there is a church run by the Capuchin friars that
is often referred to as "the Bone Church." The basement, or
crypt, of the church is decorated, floor to ceiling, with thousands of bones from deceased friars as well as those of friends

and benefactors. Some way to treat your friends! Macabre as it seems, a stroll through rooms of this church basement is also a reality check. In the last room, written on a sign in the center of the floor, is this: "What you are now, we once were. What we are now, you soon will be."

The focus of the meditations now changes significantly. Even if we were totally successful in our earlier meditation and have shifted the real horizon of our lives from death to God and eternity, death remains a real inevitability. In view of that fact, to meditate upon our own death, while appearing perhaps a bit morbid, helps us keep our priorities in line. It helps us prepare for that inevitable and unavoidable moment, and it helps us to check in on our attachments and our earthly pursuits.

When St. John Bosco founded the Salesian Society (named after St. Francis de Sales), he integrated a practice called, "Exercise for a Happy Death" into the regular spiritual routine of the order. Once per month the community has a day of recollection. They treat this day as though it were their last. They say their prayers as though it is the last time they will say them on this earth. They go to Confession as if it were their last Confession before dying. They celebrate the Mass as though it were their last celebration of that sacrifice before they come face-to-face with God. The point, of course, is to jostle themselves out of the drowsiness that comes from worldly attachment and to pray and live like every minute counts.

Ask yourself, "If I were to die today, what would I regret having done and not done?" Your answer, made in the context of our faith, should stir you to motivated activity and a savoring of what time is given you. You will die; what a blessing it would be to arrive at that day fully prepared to move from this life to the next. Facilitating that achievement is the aim of a meditation on the topic of death.

A FAREWELL TO CONTROL

We have prayed at length over the issue of our love for control. Death is truly the moment at which we lose all control. The more we have clung to control and fought for it throughout our lives, the more desperately terrifying will be that moment of our death. Again we must do battle with the inherent desire to be in control of our lives. Only when we allow that desire to be subsumed by a trusting faith are we able to embrace the fact that we are not truly in control. We can control many details of our lives and we can influence the direction of many events in our lives, but often we cling to that power. When we analyze that clinging, we typically discover that we are back to the enthroned self, as we have called it: we want control because we want to be like God. The childlike faith of so many of the saints is the fruit of moving from childishness to trust. In ultimate matters like death, the urgency is to be very realistic in our approach in order to be well prepared for our last moments on earth.

There are many stories of the great worldly figures throughout the ages, of men and women who were tremendously successful in the ways of the world: great leaders, wealthy business people, nobles and kings and queens who conquered whatever stood in their way and dominated life from beginning to end . . . or at least, almost to the end. Some of these stories tell of the final moments of such famous figures. The stories are at worst chilling and at best instructive. These masters of the world often face death in a less-than-glamorous way. Their successes and victories had taught them to believe themselves invincible or all-powerful (and so they had consequently often rejected God). In that moment of ultimate powerlessness, the calm composure that led so many people to admire and follow them through life gives way to nothing less than shrieking terror. These accounts tell of their clutching desperately at anything and everything they can reach with their hands, begging whomever is nearest to not let them go, staring off into the distance and whimpering in total fear.

Such is the final posture of one who has lived totally on the world's terms and convinced oneself that the world is their subject. Death comes to all, and to be well prepared for death is to know of its approach, not to fear but rather anticipate it. Our lives conclude in total powerlessness. What is more, not only do we rescind all control of life in the moment of our death but we also have no control over the moment God chooses for our death. Like so many other aspects of our considerations, this should be liberating rather than terrifying. It should mean living, like the Salesians, as though death could come at any moment and so not fearing it but preparing for it.

Letting go of the desire to be in total control is the beginning of all of our preparations for death. We ask God for a spirit of docility and for the grace to live each moment of life with open rather than clutching hands. When we cannot manage to rein in the human longing for control, we cannot give God the space to lead us; we remain, in our own conception, at the center of our own existence. When this is so, tragically, we limit God to interacting with us on our own terms as we refuse to accept his help in any other manner than the way we choose. Faith continually reminds us that letting go of control is not a matter of giving up but of handing over the course of our lives to One who loves us, to God who guides us and who has great plans for us: "For I know well the plans I have in mind for you . . . plans for your welfare and not for woe, so as to give you a future full of hope" (Jer 29:11).

Many paintings of the saints portray their subject sitting at a desk holding or looking at a skull. Seemingly macabre like the "Bone Church," the paintings communicate a stark reminder of the reality that these great lovers of God lived well aware always of the limits of their earthly time. The final book of the Bible reminds us, "If you are not watchful, I will come like a thief, and you will never know at what hour I will come upon you" (Rv 3:3). So let us meditate well upon our own death, and thereby remain watchful!

TIME AND ETERNITY, BODY AND SOUL

Death is the moment the soul leaves the body. We know that our souls are immortal and our bodies obviously are not. Contemplating eternity, which we shall do in several of the coming meditations, is of the utmost importance for us. Our finite minds struggle to grasp the infinite, especially because we must try to do so from within the context of what we actually understand: non-eternity, or the passage of time according to the movement of bodies. By the movement of the planets we measure time, and through the counting of days and years we measure the age of the body and thus the length of our lives. Because we start our existence here, enfleshed souls, we tend to conclude without much thought that this life is the whole story. That is our default position, with death as the horizon. Of course our faith tells us otherwise, as we have considered, but it takes a steady and graced focus to undo the default position. We begin our experience of eternity within time as measured by the movement of bodies. We must conclude our experience of time—at the moment of our death—deeply aware that our incarnate, bodily experience conditions our basic understanding of time but need not limit it. With de Sales's guidance, we will try to break those limits by relying on the fruits of the previous meditations as we ponder the reality of death.

De Sales encourages us to begin praying on this subject by imagining ourselves on our death bed with no hope of recovery. Immediately, the image of the saint holding the skull comes to mind, doesn't it? That's us.

When we die, what will it be like? Will we be alone or surrounded by family and friends? Will it be sudden and tragic or slow and expected? Will we be old or young? Winter or summer? Day or night? The more questions we ask, the more we realize we know absolutely nothing about our own death, except that it will happen and, says de Sales, probably more quickly than we would like. The importance of asking these questions which have no answers is quite simple: we must detach from the desire to control the circumstances of that moment. In a spirit of surrender to God, we ask for the grace to accept that this moment is unavoidably coming and that the best thing we can do in view of that unknown "when" is to be always ready. To live always ready to die is a great and virtuous way to be, and it takes tremendous detachment and magnificent trust.

SHIFTING OUT OF TIME AND INTO ETERNITY

For the sake of this meditation, we must take some liberty with the imagination. We often hear that, just before death, a person's whole life flashes before their eyes. Whether or not this is really the case, here we shall pretend it is so. In those final moments before the soul leaves the body, we realize the world we have known is coming to an end. Up until this very moment, we have always known reality in the context of our bodies. Suddenly, we will depart from our senses of taste, touch, smell, sound, and sight. At first scary, this thought opens us to something profound: there is much more to knowing and being than simply that which we experience through the senses.

Of course, we already know this—we know so well the power of emotions, and in particular of love, as real human experiences that occur within the body but are above and beyond the simple level of sense perception. Yet as we prepare to leave our bodies, we realize there must be another way of knowing. We realize too that we are about to enter into it completely whether we like it or not. We are also about to lose the way we measure time, which simply means we are stepping out of time as we know it. Once more, it is both scary because we have never thought of it and freeing because we realize we are about to enter into the "the real reality"; until now we have experienced reality under a particular aspect for a short period—life in the flesh—within a much greater eternity.

As we straddle this moment, we begin to understand our departure from the limits of both body and time. Our perspective shifts. We realize that there is more to reality than we often let ourselves believe and that the deepest reality is what we are about to experience. This shift makes the choices and the priorities of our bodily lives come into focus for what they really are. The things that seemed to matter so much—bodily pleasures, human praise, worldly accomplishments, money and possessions—have no meaning or value outside the framework of the material world. What seemed so real and so important now becomes almost two-dimensional, passing, and certainly unsatisfying. Immediately, we realize the silliness of having put so much value on them, and we see the sinful actions we undertook in their pursuit. We marvel at how hard we worked to achieve or accumulate and at what great lengths we went for the sake of these limited goods. They become almost translucent as we prepare to move out of the realm of the material and passing world. With shock and sadness, we see how blind we were to have prized something so simple and passing.

In the same instant, as the worldly elements of our lives lose their clarity and importance, other aspects of our lives shift into clearer focus and more textured color: our good works, the virtues, our charity and charitable acts, the effects of our faith lived out. As this shift occurs, each of us will encounter the great truth about our lives in the balance between these two. As de Sales says with stark realism, "Sins that once seemed so small will then appear as huge as mountains but your devotion very little."[2]

To live always ready to die means to strive constantly for devotion and sanctity *right now*—to tip the scales so that our good works and virtues outweigh our worldliness and self-serving ways. At the end of Graham Greene's *The Power and the Glory*, the main character faces his own death. As he does so, he reflects to himself:

> What an impossible fellow I am, he thought, and how useless. I have done nothing for anybody. I might just as well have never lived. His parents were dead—soon he wouldn't even be a memory—perhaps after all he was not at the moment afraid of damnation—even the fear of pain was in the background. He felt only an immense disappointment because he had to go to God empty-handed, with nothing done at all. It seemed to him, at that moment, that it would have been quite easy to have been a saint. It would only have needed a little self-restraint and a little courage.

> He felt like someone who has missed happiness by
> seconds at an appointed place. He knew now that at
> the end there was only one thing that counted—to
> be a saint.[3]

In the end, only one thing matters: to be a saint.

THE LONG FAREWELL

Once more allowing our imaginations to lead us, we imagine
the farewell our souls will bid to all creatures as we depart from
this formal connection to God's material creation. We will say
farewell to our relationships with a keen awareness of which
ones helped and which ones hurt. We leave behind all of our
possessions with a deep knowledge of which ones assisted and
which ones impeded us on our journey to this moment. We
take one last glance at our work, our hobbies, our recreation,
at food, drink, song, and dance. We allow our minds to linger
over all of our choices and can see now more clearly than ever
where we served ourselves in them and where we served others.
The shock of perspective allows us to analyze and evaluate every
relationship, undertaking, acquisition, and pursuit in a single
glance. All that harmed us shifts to black and white, and all that
aided comes into full color. This is because eternity—and the
possibility of eternal bliss—is the lens through which we now
see. Had we seen this way during life, we would certainly have
opted for color rather than gray. This is why, in this present life,
we must strive so ardently to shift horizons.

In one last glance, we will say farewell to our bodies. The body falls into lifelessness, losing color and warmth. Quickly, it becomes a chilling sight both for us and for those around it. For those still living who behold this now lifeless body, it becomes simply a shadow and a memory of the one they loved. For us, as we look back in departure, it chills us to behold the body because only now do we realize its true importance. So often, especially in our youth, we place such great value upon appearance. At times, this shifts into the obsessive concern we call vanity. At the other end of the spectrum, of course, is carelessness, disrespect, and ultimately abuse of the body. As Aristotle said, the virtue lies in the mean.[4] To look upon our bodies with peace at our passing, we must presently live an important balance. We must see the body as a gift from God, unique and truly beautiful. Not beautiful in the way that so often Hollywood or the media portray the body, objectifying it, but beautiful in terms of its God-willed importance as "us," the flesh by which the soul knew and made itself known in life. The body is a temple, not to be abused or neglected and not to be obsessively adorned. Should we be guilty of either extreme, we will look upon it in sadness as we depart. We will suffer the deep awareness that we either failed to cherish a gift or that we abused the gift for passing pleasure and pointless vanity.

It is important to temper our tendency to obsess over our bodies by considering the next moments as well. Just a few moments after our death, our bodies will be quickly rushed off and prepared for burial. Ashes to ashes, dust to dust. Our bodies will be quickly buried, prayers said, and the planet keeps spinning. Evening comes, and morning follows . . . the next day.

Immediately, we are no longer part of the worldly lives of those we knew in our time. Quickly, we will fade from the memory of so many. The only ones who will remember us are those whom we have loved and who have loved us . . . really loved. Aristotle spoke of the various types of friendship, naming three of them:[5] there are friendships of utility, where the friends mutually benefit one another for some further gain; there are friendships of pleasure, where the friends enjoy one another's company; and there are true friendships, where the friends value one another for the sake of the goodness of the other. Those coworkers and colleagues of utility, those party friends or gossip circles, any relationships of the first two types will but remember us occasionally, remembering the good times and wistfully moving on. Our worldly accomplishments, even if they are many, will not bring us any benefit at this point nor will the memory of "us" that may or may not live on, though we spend much of our lives energetically hoping to make such a mark.

For example, who can recall the name of the world's richest person from twenty-five years ago? Of course, we remember the names of presidents and generals, revolutionaries and writers, but such a memory does not benefit them any longer. More important, it actually only benefits us if it calls us to a pursuit of higher things.

Those who will truly remember us are those whom we have brought to a better place by our friendship and those by whom we have been brought to a better place. A real friend seeks the good of the other, his or her perfection. In the context of ultimate reality, the greatest perfection of the human person is eternal communion with God forever in heaven. True friends are those who take us closer to that place and for whom we have sought to do the same. As the Irish prayer goes, "Pray for me as I will for thee, that we may merrily meet in heaven!" These are the ones who will remember us, have Masses said for us, cry in our absence, speak to us in prayer, carry our picture with them, and tell stories about us. We must consider these important facts not because we want to be remembered once we die but to stress the importance of truly good relationships and to give all that we have to living them in a real, Christian, charity-imbued way here and now.

FREEDOM FROM FEAR

Death is not an easy subject! Perhaps for this reason we do not consider it more freely and frequently. For most of us, the thought of death usually stirs up some form of anxiety or fear. What is perhaps most terrifying about death is simply the fact that what lies beyond is seemingly unknown. At the very deepest level, we long for communion, to love and be loved, to be a part of the human family. We are made for love! Death seems to be the final departure from the human family, when we enter into a loneliness and isolation that is apparently total. If we let death remain in this darkness, we will always fear it.

The essential truths of our faith empty this fear, and radically so. The communion to which we are called, indeed for which we are made, is more profound and complete than even anything we could experience here in this life. In our time here, every joy, every love, every communion is simply a foretaste of what is potentially to come. No matter how perfect and joyful it may be, life here is punctuated by sin: even though "the just fall seven times, they rise again" (Prv 24:16). Our communion and love here, certainly blessed and wonderful but incomplete and imperfect, stirs up a greater ardor for that which is to come. Heaven is ultimate, eternal and unbroken communion with God and with the angels and saints. We will consider this later in more detail, but for now we must allow faith, hope, and love to lift us out of the fear of death. Death is simply a passing point, from intermittent communion into, please God, perfect communion.

In the meantime, we are free: free to strive for the best communion possible here and now; free to choose holy, lasting friendships; free to pursue the good, to live well and virtuously, and to strive for all that is eternally colorful. By the grace of God, we discern the way that will lead us to a greater and deeper fullness. By his help, nurtured by the sacraments and prayer, we avoid all that would ensnare us and tie us down. The sincere awareness of our death and its unknown approach frees us from becoming overly concerned with worldly pursuits and possessions. Power, pleasure, honor, and wealth are all goods . . . but they are not the ultimate good.

FOCUS FOR THE DAY'S PRAYER

Embrace the gift of your freedom in gratitude and awareness of the passage of time. Consider the importance of real, faithful relationships. Ask yourself where you cling to material or passing things and where you cling to control. Prayerfully, constantly, consider the inevitable reality of your death. Ask God's grace in reorienting and reordering your whole life toward charity, love of God, and love of neighbor. Ask for the grace to waste not a moment of the time given to you by God before that reality arrives.

———

Lord God, grant me always the grace to live each and every moment as if it were my last. Help me always to set my gaze upon eternity and to cherish the flow of each earthly moment as one filled with your presence. Help me to see the time allotted to me here and now as a blessed chance to glorify you and to praise you by imitating Christ and living the Gospel. Help me always to live in a state of readiness, knowing neither the day nor the hour. And please, Oh God, grant me the gift of a happy death and a peaceful passing into the fullness of your embrace. Amen.

THE SIXTH MEDITATION:
On Judgment

Detest your sins for they alone can ruin you on
that dreadful day. Ah, I will judge myself now
so that I may not be judged! I will examine my
conscience and condemn, accuse, and amend
myself so that the Judge will not condemn me.[1]

Place yourself in the presence of God.
Ask him to inspire you.

We resume precisely where we concluded in the previous meditation. Once the soul's long farewell is complete, it proceeds on its journey. The journey has two alternative destinations: heaven or hell. No, we do not like to talk about these much anymore, especially because they bear such radical implications on our present and cause a lot of discomfort or even conflict in contemporary conversation. Before we consider heaven and hell, we must consider the topic of God's judgment, a topic remarkably absent from many of today's "religious" conversations. Before we can begin praying over the subject, we need a little philosophy, some scripture, and a bit of assistance from the *Catechism of the Catholic Church*.

Often times, we find ourselves thinking about the Church's teaching on judgment and condemnation as a human ingenuity designed simply to keep everyone in line, to scare us into obedience. Today, when someone brings up the topic, they might be accused of being a bit too traditional or old-school in their Catholicism. The image of Christ the Judge gives way to images such as the laughing Jesus. Certainly, we are in a profound relationship of brotherhood with Jesus Christ in virtue of our Baptism. Furthermore, as Jesus was fully human, he certainly must have laughed, smiled, and joked with his friends. These facts call us to a deeply familiar and truly friendly relationship with Jesus. Perhaps the best model of prayer ever proposed in the history of the Catholic faith is that of St. Teresa of Avila, who said that we should think of prayer as nothing other than friendly, intimate conversation with God, who we know loves us.[2] Friendship with God is an essential aspect of our relationship with him and one to which we all must have recourse in our own interior lives.

However, none of this eliminates the fact that Christ spoke of himself as judge and referenced the final judgment at the end of time. Perhaps not an exciting topic, God's judgment is an unavoidable one: first, because it is an essential part of our

Catholic faith; and second, relevant to our present purpose, because de Sales insists that we spend an entire meditation on the topic.

FREEDOM'S WEIGHT

We have already considered the great importance of fully understanding human freedom. If we hold that we are truly free to make choices, we are in fact making a bigger statement than we might realize. Provided we accept the existence of an immortal soul and an afterlife, when we make statements about human freedom we in fact also make statements about heaven and hell. How so? Well, the opposite of freedom is determinism, which argues that everything is already determined. In fact, we cannot argue that we are genuinely and totally free while also arguing that there is no hell. If our place in heaven is already determined then our choices here are not truly free because they do not have any force over our final destination; while we could argue for a modified concept of freedom within a determined final outcome, it would not be authentic freedom as it cannot change anything about the conclusion. Genuine freedom means we are completely free to choose and to make choices that have an eternal bearing. Ultimately, freedom means we are free to choose our eternal residence—either with God or without God. These eternal realities are the subject of the next two meditations. Because both eternal realities exist, and because it would be sheer madness to claim that any human tribunal could have the authority to determine a soul's final destination, we logically acknowledge that there must be some higher Judge. If logic is not enough to satisfy us, we have God's Word, which speaks to us on the matter.

JUSTICE, THE JUDGE, AND JUDGMENT

God has revealed to us that, at the end of time, Christ will judge between the living and the dead (Rv 20:11–15, 21:5–8). The scriptures contain manifold references to this fact, often in the very words of Christ himself. The *Catechism of the Catholic Church* summarizes: "Following in the steps of the prophets and John the Baptist, Jesus announced the judgment of the Last Day in his preaching" (*CCC*, 678).

Page through John's gospel, Paul's letters, or the book of Revelation; they are loaded with references. In Matthew's gospel, we find perhaps the most concise yet complete summary on the topic. De Sales uses it to ground our meditation:

> When the Son of Man comes in his glory, and all the angels with him, he will sit upon his glorious throne, and all the nations will be assembled before him. And he will separate them one from another, as a shepherd separates the sheep from the goats. He will place the sheep on his right and the goats on his left. Then the king will say to those on his right, "Come, you who are blessed by my Father. Inherit the kingdom prepared for you from the foundation of the world." . . . Then he will say to those on

> his left, "Depart from me, you accursed, into the
> eternal fire prepared for the devil and his angels".
> . . and these will go off to eternal punishment, but
> the righteous to eternal life. (Mt 25:31–34, 41, 46)

Two fundamental passages from the *Catechism* explain the foundation of the Church's teaching on these matters and must be set out before we can prayerfully begin considering the subject of judgment. First, referring to the Last Day, the *Catechism* says, "Then will the conduct of each one and the secrets of hearts be brought to light. Then will the culpable unbelief that counted the offer of God's grace as nothing be condemned. Our attitude about our neighbor will disclose acceptance or refusal of grace and divine love. On the last day Jesus will say: 'Truly I say to you, as you did it to one of the least of these my brethren, you did it to me'" (*CCC*, 678).

The *Catechism* goes on to refer to Christ as the Judge of the living and the dead: "Christ is the Lord of eternal life. Full right to pass definitive judgment on the works and hearts of men belongs to him as redeemer of the world. He 'acquired' this right by his cross. The Father has given 'all judgment to the Son.' Yet the Son did not come to judge, but to save and to give the life he has in himself. By rejecting grace in this life, one already judges oneself, receives according to one's works, and can even condemn oneself for all eternity by rejecting the Spirit of love" (*CCC*, 679).

Justice is the virtue of rendering unto another that which is their due. As we have considered previously, our freely chosen actions are not neutral: they have merit as well as consequences. Christ's judgment is not out of anger or vengeance but is rather a judgment that renders to each what is their due; he judges us according to our deeds, or rather he passes the judgment that is the logical conclusion of our choices.

Finally, while conversation about Christ's judgment may make us feel uncomfortable, we always hold in tension the great and beautiful gift of knowing he is both a just and merciful judge. God's mercy is somewhat mysterious to us, and in the great hopefulness of our faith we entrust our own lives and the souls of all of the faithful departed to that mercy without presuming anything. In striving to live like Christ, and along the way of conversion, we must always carefully resist the temptation to play Christ's role and judge others. Though we know the categories of good and evil, we cannot see into the hearts of others to understand all of the circumstances that lead them to choose as they do. On the topic of God's mercy, we recognize the fact that the Catholic Church has never proclaimed definitively that anyone is in hell. We simply do not know. What we do know is that hell is real and a real possibility of human freedom is that we could find ourselves there for eternity. This possibility grounds our meditations and gives us the material to pray into a greater resolve as we strive to avoid hell and to help others do so as well.

A NEW CREATION
AND THE JUDGMENT SEAT

We have prayed at length about the importance of a healthy detachment from created or material realities. Such detachment aids us in contemplating our death and in stirring a longing for eternal blessedness. More broadly, we know that creation itself is passing away; it is not the completed reality of God's final plan but rather a work in progress. As we read in Revelation 21, on the last day a new creation will replace the former heaven and earth. In the preceding chapter, John speaks of the Judgment: "I saw the dead, the great and the lowly, standing before the throne. . . . The dead were judged according to their deeds" (Rv 20:12). This, finally, is where our prayer begins.

We must once more use prayerfully guided imagination to enter into the contents of the meditation. At the end of time, Christ will appear radiant in full glory, seated on the judgment throne. This full revelation of his power and majesty will lead all to worship him: "Whenever the living creatures give glory and honor and thanks to the one who sits on the throne, who lives forever and ever, the twenty-four elders fall down before the one who sits on the throne and worship him, who lives forever and ever. They throw down their crowns before the throne, exclaiming, 'Worthy are you, Lord our God, to receive glory and honor and power, for you created all things; because of your will they came to be and were created'" (Rv 4:9–11).

His radiance we recall from the Transfiguration, when he allowed the veil of his flesh to be drawn back and his full divinity to be revealed. At the end of time, when he comes to judge the living and the dead, he will be all in all, Alpha and Omega, triumphant over the last uprising of evil. His glory shall be totally unveiled, and as the dead appear before him, they will know the time for judgment has arrived. The Cross will stand before him as his standard, and it will shine as the instrument of our salvation, his victory over sin and death. It will draw the gaze and hearts of those who honored it with their lives, and it will terrify those who have spurned or rejected it.

Then, at his word, Christ will separate the sheep from the goats. They will be separated forever by a great chasm never to be crossed (see Lk 16:26), for this judgment is final. As the two are separated, the good from the evil, the difference will be astoundingly clear. The good, gathered now together, will shine with the radiance of God himself, and the evil will groan and gnash their teeth in anguish. In our prayer, as bystanders to such a judgment, no imagery is too graphic or extensive to emphasize the mighty distance between the two. Hearts will be exposed, and all will be laid bare as Christ foretold: "There is nothing concealed that will not be revealed, nor secret that will not be known. Therefore whatever you have said in the darkness will be heard in the light, and what you have whispered behind closed doors will be proclaimed on the housetops" (Lk 12:2–3).

THE WICKED AND THE GOOD

The defining feature of the wicked will be their hatred for God. Their faces will bear many similarities to the expressions we often notice in our present day. Hatred for God shows itself in many forms, perhaps many more than we realize. Militant atheism, of course, is the most obvious. More subtle are the various forms of humanism that do not directly attack God but elevate humanity to the level of God and thus replace him. Materialism, individualism, relativism, and hedonism are all features of the present age that destroy the roots of charity within the soul. They eventually undermine our relationship with God enough to lead to at least a passive and sometimes direct opposition to God.

Evil is only visibly manifest when the devil deems the matter urgent, such as when a great good is at hand that, in evil terms, must be opposed. Much more frequently, we encounter the working of evil under the cover of subtlety and thus so often miss its movements; the evil one works most effectively in gradually urging hearts away from love of God first into tepidity and finally into distaste and hatred. Excessive love for created things, idolatry, and the selfishness of lust are but a few ways that the evil one leads us to deface the image of God in ourselves and others; it always happens in small steps that lead to greater ones. Revelation 21:8 speaks of "cowards, the unfaithful, the depraved, murderers, the unchaste, sorcerers, idol-worshipers, and deceivers of every sort." Few of these set out at the beginning to hate God; most started with small denials of God that grew like weeds and choked his life in them.

In contrast, "What came to be through him was life, and this life was the light of the human race; the light shines in the darkness, and the darkness has not overcome it" (Jn 1:3–5). The defining feature of the good will be the shining fruit of their repentance and the splendor of their good deeds. God's grace will shine through and around those who are now gathered together. They have overcome the snares of evil and persevered in grace and goodness. Unlike anything we have seen before, the intense splendor of goodness shines radiantly as these holy ones gather into a single community. The light of goodness is an almost startling affirmation of the soul-peace that comes from rejecting evil and living as members of the kingdom of God.

THE FINAL WORD

Beholding the scene of the final judgment in the sanctuary of our prayer, we remember that what we see is the coming of a new creation as the old has passed away. We do not have, from our own experience, images or knowledge of the precise details of what this looks like. However, we allow the Lord to lead us in contemplating once more the vast distance between the groups he has separated in this final judgment.

We listen attentively as we hear the final words of the Judge to each group. To the wicked, he says, "Depart from me, you accursed, into the eternal fire prepared for the devil and his angels" (Mt 25:41). In a covenant relationship, those who uphold the requirements of the covenant receive a blessing, and those who violate it receive a curse. In life, those who rejected God's grace reject the covenant relationship to which he calls them; they thus invoke a curse upon themselves. On the final day, that curse is eternal as they are cast from the presence of God forever. The finality of that word rings in our own hearts as we consider this judgment. In our prayer, we must imagine the terror this word would inflict on our soul as we see the light of eternal joy fade. The wicked turn forever from such hope and face an eternity of flames. What greater agony could there be than to come before God himself and hear the sound of rejection! De Sales urges us: "Weigh well those heavy words. . . . O my soul, what a curse. . . . Behold, O my heart, that vast eternity! O eternal eternity of pain, how dreadful thou art!"[3]

To the righteous, he says, "Come, you blessed ones, inherit the kingdom!" (see Mt 25:34). The thought of entering the kingdom of God once and for all lifts the heart. This eternal kingdom is finally the state of being wherein sadness, division, and pain slip away and peace, union, and goodness take their place. We cannot over-emphasize this in our prayer, for nothing we have ever known in this life could compare to the joy we should know at hearing these words: the blessing of all blessings, the "sweet word of salvation by which God draws us to himself and receives us into the bosom of his goodness."[4]

At that moment before God, we will hear a statement that is entirely eternal—heaven or hell. Our present consideration of the finality of these last words must shake us to our core. In

life, we have known nothing to be of such finality. Even the evil
we choose freely in life is undone by grace and forgiveness. It
requires great patience and a true stretching of the mind and
heart to contemplate the eternal finality we consider here. As has
been so fruitful previously, we look back on our own sinful past.
We note that the one thing that would lead us to destruction on
that final day is persistence in our sinful ways.

Deeply aware of this reality, we once more detest our past
sins and accuse ourselves of having committed them. We do so
to rid ourselves of these sins and purge our affinity for them,
lest with time we return to walking the gradual decline into the
mire of our past. In all prayerful prudence, we consider that
acts of penance, prayer, fasting, and almsgiving can all serve to
strengthen our resolve and make amends for our past sinfulness. Contemplating the stark reality of our own final judgment
assists us in further sealing our good intentions, while it also
strengthens our resolve to develop that quickness of spirit to act
virtuously. We recognize that everything, absolutely everything,
is at stake. Without knowing the moment of our death, we hear
St. Gregory of Nazianzen's challenge: "Let there be no delay
between your good intention and your good deed."[5]

Finally, in great peace and joy, we take tremendous confidence in knowing that our judgment is not this day. At the same
time, we resist any temptation to put off further repentance.
Moreover, we rejoice in a simple but amazingly beautiful fact:
God has already given us absolutely everything we need, by
grace and by sacrament, to ensure that we need never hear those

words of condemnation! We ought to always give thanks for this important fact, lest we take it for granted and fail to respond with the fullness of our freedom in striving for the good.

Above all else, in the act of considering this heavy subject, we recognize the eternal goodness of God himself and we remind ourselves that his only desire is for our eternal happiness. He has already extended the offer and has been hard at work every moment of every day to make this a reality. It is up to us to respond in freedom, joy, and faith.

FOCUS FOR THE DAY'S PRAYER

Carry in your heart a deeper awareness of the basic fact that you will be judged based on your actions and omissions. Consider that reality throughout the day. Trust in God's mercy, but know of his justice. All that is evil moves you away from love of God toward a place of despair and sadness. Watch carefully today for those movements.

Pray with the very finality of the moment of final judgment, considering that once the judgment is rendered, nothing can ever undo or change it. Ask God to help you long more fully to be among the elect who "will shine like the sun in the kingdom of their Father" (Mt 13:43); ask for a new ardor and zeal; and ask God to help you live consciously aware of that final moment and to begin in haste to "store up treasures in heaven" (Mt 6:20).

Lord God, Almighty Father, thank you for the deepening awareness to which you are bringing me—self-awareness and awareness of your love for me. Thank you also for all that you have done, all that you are doing, and all that you will do to safeguard me from the pitfalls and temptations that would ensnare me. Help me to do penance and to amend my life. I beg you to increase your gifts of faith, hope, and love in me so I may spend myself loving, honoring, and glorifying you by my life. Amen.

THE SEVENTH MEDITATION:

On Hell

Strike terror into your soul by the words of
Isaiah: "O my soul, how can you dwell with this
everlasting burning and in this devouring fire?"
How can you think of parting from God forever?[1]

Place yourself in the presence of God.
Ask him to inspire you.

If the topic of judgment causes some contemporary resistance,
then meditation on hell causes downright opposition. In quite
a few ways, hell has become a topic we would much prefer to
avoid in conversation as well as contemplation. Our logic tends
to work like this: "If God is really the God of love then he could
not possibly allow someone to go to hell, and so hell could not
be real. It must be another fabrication the Church has conjured
up to keep us in line." However, in the movie *The Usual Suspects*,

near the end of the film, the main character sums up a chilling truth: "The greatest trick the devil ever pulled was convincing the world he didn't exist."[2] We know by God's revelation and by our experience of evil in the world that Satan does exist, and we recognize that it would be the devil's victory were we to cease to believe in him and all his works.

To contemplate hell, once again we have to recall that damnation does not come about because God delights in punishing or inflicting pain. Remember the previous meditation: God wants nothing but our good, but he is a just Judge. By our freedom we are able to exclude ourselves from his goodness. Pray with the words of John's gospel:

> For God so loved the world that he gave his only Son, so that everyone who believes in him might not perish but might have eternal life. For God did not send his Son into the world to condemn the world, but that the world might be saved through him. Whoever believes in him will not be condemned, but whoever does not believe has already been condemned, because he has not believed in the name of the only Son of God. And this is the verdict, that the light came into the world, but people preferred darkness to light, because their works were evil. For everyone who does wicked things hates the light and does not come toward the light, so that his works might not be exposed. But whoever lives the truth comes to the light, so that his works may be clearly seen as done in God. (3:16–21)

The Church defines hell as the, "state of definitive self-exclusion from communion with God and the blessed" (*CCC*, 1033). The great Christian hope is that by God's mercy none may have to suffer eternal sadness. Yet because we know the full potential of human freedom, we now turn our thoughts toward that eternal sadness. This will be our most challenging meditation; we pray that God will grant us the insights we need and nothing more, and we pray to our guardian angels to be with us that this meditation may lead us to deeper conversion and, ultimately, greater love of God.

THE GRAY CITY OF SADNESS

Imagine a city, huge and sprawling. A great and endless smog hangs over this city, a place with no color and no music. Its people never see the sun shine. Its summer is gray and always too hot, and its winter gray and always too cold. The city reeks with the stench of sulfur, sweat, and sadness. There are no windows or doors to block out the heavy air and no real privacy in which to hide from the constant dreariness of life. No laughter is ever heard in the streets of this city, only the sound of wailing, discomfort, angst, and anxiety. There is no clean water and never enough food, and yet nobody dies. This city's name is Despair. Death would be a welcome end, but it has no place in this city. Most awfully, everyone in this city remembers what it was like to live in a better place. Worst of all, nobody in this city will ever leave.

Images like this are, of course, exaggerated but necessary. When we contemplate eternal realities such as heaven and hell, we step out of the realm of our real understanding and experience. To consider hell, we must move to an extreme and create an image for ourselves that somehow captures a hint of what such an eternal reality would be like. In all truth, our wildest imaginations cannot embrace the full terror of damnation. We grasp at a glimmer of that state of being by cobbling together our own experiences to provide an imaginary taste of something so awful. To draw this out, we will look at suffering on several levels before concluding with a brief reflection on eternity.

THE SUFFERING OF THE SENSES

De Sales first invites us to meditate on the sufferings of the senses that hell would bring. Though our bodies remain in the earth after death, we know that at the end of time body will be reunited with soul, and so we first consider the experience of an eternal physical suffering.

In such a state of being, every sense would suffer, perhaps in proportion to the use that was made of that sense to enjoy the illicit pleasures of sinfulness during earthly life. Our sight would be filled with terrifying and gruesome images from which we cannot turn our gaze. Our ears, always open, would only hear weeping and screams. Our bodies would experience constant discomfort. We would always be hungry and never satisfied, always thirsty and never quenched. Sleep would not exist, though we would remember it and long for it. We could not stretch our limbs, if such stretching would bring peace. We could not sit, if sitting would relax us. Any bodily comfort would be but a memory to remind us of the depths of this present—and endless—discomfort. Spend time considering the greatest physical discomforts of your life; then imagine that they all happen at once and in greater intensity than ever before.

EMOTIONAL AND SPIRITUAL SUFFERING

As though bodily suffering were not enough, the soul would also suffer. Any and every enjoyable emotion would be just a painful memory. Whatever our worst fears and most dreaded emotions may be, these would crowd our present forever: sadness, loneliness, self-loathing, paranoia, angst, despair. We would remember what it was like to be free of the burden of these emotions, and we would recall the happiness we had in their absence. Such a memory would multiply the weight of our sadness.

Far worse than emotional suffering would be spiritual suffering: "The chief punishment of hell is eternal separation from God, in whom alone man can possess the life and happiness for which he was created and for which he longs" (*CCC*, 1035). Truth, goodness, and beauty in life lift us up out of ourselves and into God. For this reason, we call them the "transcendentals"—they help us to transcend the limits of our experience of reality and enter into contemplating and experiencing its eternal fullness. These, and our experience of them, would have no place in hell. Nor would there be a place for the peace they once brought. In fact, all peace would be gone. Any joy, tranquility, harmony, or communion would be shattered, leaving no rest whatsoever for the soul.

ETERNAL SUFFERING

We might conclude and summarize these considerations by drawing more concretely from our own experience. In our imagination, we place together all of the most awful experiences of our lives and unite them with all of our worst fears, our greatest failures, and our darkest emotions. If we could distill this terrible combination into a single experience of desolation, it would still be far too small to capture the pain of hell. Why? Because no matter what our suffering in this life, no matter how great the pain or sadness or fear, our afflictions are always tempered by the knowledge and the hope that, eventually, the suffering will pass.

We can endure a lot of discomfort when we know it will eventually come to an end, but in the eternity of hell, no longer would the sufferings of our existence be punctuated by the joys of living. Only sadness and agony would remain. The memory of joy and happiness would harden that sadness. The deep knowledge that this state is eternal would torment us beyond imagination.

By far the greatest sadness of hell would be the sadness of knowing that we will never see God, never know his love, never receive his embrace, never know the peace of soul that comes from grace. Such sadness would be deepened by the awareness that we chose this eternal desolation for ourselves by rejecting his grace and by failing to repent. Perhaps we would remember all of the moments he approached us, called us back, invited us to conversion. Perhaps we would resent ourselves ever more for each and every reproach we uttered, every spurning of grace, every twist of pride by which we said we were fine on our own, that we did not need God or any of his help. The delights we derived from our sinful pursuits would now appear so miniscule, and we would see that we traded the passing pleasures of earthly indulgence for the endless agony of eternal damnation.

THE MADNESS OF IT ALL

We need not linger long on these thoughts before we realize their awful possibilities. We would have to be mad to choose such an eternity! Here we encounter the purpose of this meditation: to force us to imagine the awful state of eternity that remains a possibility for us. Given the opportunity to stand on the brink of hell, behold all we would undergo there, and make a choice, we would never choose it. Yet hell is not a one-time choice for us, at least not for most. Eternal damnation is generally a gradual choice, one made by a thousand smaller choices. Our deeds judge us.

The gradual choice begins with the basic sinful movements of our lives: pride, envy, lust, anger, and jealousy; movements that creep into our hearts and lead us to break down the communion we are called to live. It grows in directional force as we fail to repent and as the conscience is hardened until it can no longer feel the twinge of guilt that sin brings. The gradual choice becomes nearly final when we find ourselves so mired in sin that we no longer give God any room in our lives. When we fail to repent and receive his grace and mercy, particularly through a regular sacramental rhythm, we have chosen to live our lives totally outside of God's grace. If we do not choose to break out of that miserable state, and as a result if we die unrepentant, our choice is final and our eternal destiny decided. Christ himself begged us not to go this way: "This is the time of fulfillment. The kingdom of God is at hand. Repent, and believe in the gospel" (Mk 1:15).

For this reason above all, de Sales calls us—again and again—to deepen the ardor of our conversion by looking at our own past sinfulness. Only our sin can lead us to hell; knowledge of our weakness strengthens our ability to avoid it. We cannot be too careful in protecting ourselves against the effects of sin we have all inherited. Every major rejection of goodness began in some small one. To put a foot on the wrong path is to risk arriving at the end of that path. Contemplation of the awful possibility of hell quickens our efforts to long more fully for the life of grace.

FOCUS FOR THE DAY'S PRAYER

Return throughout the day to the sense of agony that the imagery of hell presents. Each time something goes wrong today, or you encounter any sadness or despair, remind yourself that in this life such trials are passing but in the next they are not. Each time you encounter joy or peace today, imagine what it would be like never to experience it again. Remember that any evil is evil, no matter how small or great, and that anything opposed to faith, hope, or charity can only lead you toward eternal despair. Ask the Lord to keep these realizations at the surface of your heart so that constantly, daily, you can choose to do the good and avoid evil.

————

Dear God, patient and loving Father, I have chosen time and again to reject your goodness, preferring myself to you. By your goodness through this time of prayer, you are leading me to understand the weight of my past choices and the power you have given me in freedom. I dread nothing more than spending eternity without you. Please, I beg you, be generous now in pouring forth your assistance as I strive to spend every moment of this life in pursuing your will. Help me to live according to the truth of my being and to exist for the praise of your glory. Protect me against every temptation and every evil impulse, that when you determine the time for my departure, I may run joyfully into your embrace! Amen.

THE EIGHTH MEDITATION:
On Paradise

Fervently aspire to this most delightful abode.
My good and sovereign Lord, since it has pleased
you to direct my steps into your ways, nevermore
will I turn away from them. Let us go forward,
my dear soul, to that infinite repose, let us travel
on to that blessed land which is promised to us.[1]

Place yourself in the presence of God.
Ask him to inspire you.

We have made the two most difficult meditations of the entire journey, and we thereby crest the hill to turn now to the apex: heaven. The depth and darkness of the previous meditation quickly gives way as its opposite becomes our focus. Our method here is essentially the same as before but inverted: when

contemplating hell we considered sadness; in contemplating
heaven we consider joy.

TO SEE HEAVEN

First and foremost, we must undertake the crucial work of
purifying our notion of heaven. We have heard of heaven since
we were young. When we were children, we imagined heaven
and heard stories about that place above the clouds where the
angels live. For most of us, many of these images linger. Think
of heaven yourself and note the first images that come to mind:
clouds, the pearly gates, wings, haloes, and harps. The problem
is this: nothing about that imagery draws us to long for that
type of reality. Nobody wants to spend eternity standing on
a cloud dressed in white and holding a harp. Here we find a
major and vital disconnect. We know we are made for heaven,
and we are supposed to live for it here and now. However, when
we intentionally consider heaven, due to the limited imagery
we often carry from our childhoods, we may find that we are
not attracted by the idea of actually being there. This certainly
makes it hard to really want to live for heaven, does it not? This
movement of correcting our idea of heaven is one of the most
important works of faith we can ever undertake, for ourselves
and for as many others as possible.

To purify our notion of heaven and attempt to truly contemplate such an eternal existence, once more we call upon the
imagination. We use what we know of the world to lead us into
considering that which lies beyond our experience. As before,

the richest imagination cannot plumb the depths of the reality, but it matters that we try.

Imagine the most beautiful landscape the mind can assemble. Every detail is absolute perfection. The horizon is filled with snow-capped mountains, from which flow torrents of rushing rivulets that meet in a lush green valley to widen out and form a perfect, tranquil, flowing river. It waters every kind of flower and tree that punctuates the grassy expanse as far as the eye can see. The air is crystal clear, filled with the songs of birds and the pungent smell of every fragrant flower in perfect harmony. Now, allow some creative liberty: somehow, at one and the same time, every single star and every planet are visible in fullness. From the perfect landscape, the heart is lifted upward into the enormity of the heavens and the splendor of the galaxy, all visible and overwhelming and delightful at once.

Add to this unbelievable scene whatever you must; be as creative as you possibly can to depict the most beautiful moment imaginable. This could never compare to the beauty of the heavens. Whatever we might imagine is, we know, passing. Clouds can block the stars, fire can destroy the meadow, and an earthquake can topple the mountains. All of creation's beauty, by God's design, lifts the heart of the beholder, but it can never completely capture the perfection toward which it tends. Created beauty is passing, where heaven's is eternal. How much more beautiful would be whatever we behold if we knew, in the beholding, it was actually perfect—not just perfect to our own preferences but objectively so? How much more beautiful would it be if we knew this beauty could never fade or decay? Such, in a glimpse, would be the bliss of seeing heaven.

HEAVEN'S INHABITANTS

Beyond the physical beauty is the beauty of the community of heaven. Because we only see the earthly end of things, we often forget that the entire created order includes more than just the earth; it includes "the heavens," along with the angels, neither of which we can really understand perfectly. There are cherubim and seraphim, choirs of angels who surround the throne of God and rejoice in him eternally. How beautiful would they appear to our simple eyes? These pure spirits sing in endless praise, honoring God by their whole existence, spotless and glorious. To see them would be to see creatures whose whole existence is rooted so deeply in praise of God that they never leave the heavens. They share with us a purpose—to exist for the praise of God's glory—yet they spend their whole existence in God's presence without interruption.

Next, in our prayer, we picture all those holy ones from the vision in the book of Revelation: "a great multitude, which no one could count, from every nation, race, people, and tongue. They stood before the throne and before the Lamb, wearing white robes and holding palm branches" (7:9). With these we could perhaps identify more closely, for they are the ones who have walked the pathways of the earth as we do. In seeing them our hearts would leap, as well, for we would be seeing with our own eyes the fulfillment of our purpose. These are the ones who have triumphed, who have entered by the "narrow door" (see Lk 13:24) and come at last to the heavenly homeland, the true kingdom. Their appearance, as well, would be beautiful beyond beauty, for they would bear perfection now. We would want more than anything to be near them, like them, one with them.

ULTIMATE PERFECTION

As we allow the scene to unfold before our mind's prayerful eye, we have to recall a philosophical fact: if in God there is no imperfection then imperfection has no place in heaven. Heaven is simply the state of being in which creation is perfectly in communion with God. Imperfection cannot join perfection or the union is partial; thus, if a creature is in heaven, either it possesses no imperfection or it has been purified of all imperfection.

What does this mean for our vision of heaven? It means everything we behold in this prayerful reflection on heaven is pure and free of any imperfection. We have never seen something like this; we have never beheld created beings with no imperfections. The purity of what we see would shock us. It would capture our gaze in utter fascination and stir the most profound longing. It would be as though seeing a perfect dream while knowing it is far more real than life itself. Yet what would draw forth the very deepest cry of our nature would be the soul-stirring wonder of seeing the perfect communion the blessed share with God and one another.

As we have already considered several times, we are created for communion. Nobody wants to be alone, as we find peace and joy in loving and being genuinely loved. We are called, by vocation, to love and so imitate and encounter God. Harmony speaks to us at the soul-level of being and existence: right communion brings peace, contentment, and happiness, while broken communion causes displeasure, unease, discomfort, and tension.

In heaven, no relation is marred by jealousy, mistrust, selfishness, pride, or lust. Every single relation is perfect communion imbued with true and total charity. Most beautiful of all is the fact that this communion is bound up eternally in the ultimate communion with creation's very source, the Alpha and the Omega: God. Whatever this would truly look like, we cannot imagine, but we would see the vast multitude of all creation at its apex: perfect, victorious, complete, and glorious. The harmony of the entire heavenly reality is impossible for the finite human mind to imagine. Absolutely nothing in all existence could be more pleasing.

ETERNAL HAPPINESS

Just as we did for hell, we do for heaven. Imagine the greatest day you could ever put together. All of your closest friends gather for a surprise birthday party. The weather is perfect, the setting ideal, and the celebration sublime. You experience real, constant, authentic, and unconditional love from everyone as well as genuine peace, absolute tranquility with an overflowing sense of blessedness beyond your wildest imagination. Take that assembly of feelings, multiply it beyond quantity and stretch it beyond time, and you have barely touched upon the hem of the garment of eternal bliss. We cannot get our minds around the concept of unending joy because, in putting together the perfect day filled with the greatest joy, our human experience tells us something very real: it will end. No matter how wonderful a day you might imagine, you know it is only a day. Truly, we cannot imagine what it would be like to exist in surpassing joy and to do so without end. We can only prayerfully imagine and ask the Lord to stir in us the deepest longing for such bliss and for the grace to live in its pursuit.

One of the most life-giving fruits of these meditations is the change in how we view heaven. Heaven cannot be a distant choice or a far-off idea. It must be an ultimate goal that is on our minds constantly. In growing faith, we frequently turn our minds to this subject in order that the God-willed horizon of our existence might pour forth into our current reality to influence each moment of the present. We do so intentionally because, in the face of the present busyness of our lives and the many pressing matters that demand our attention, it can be so easy to forget the invisible, seemingly distant, but life-altering reality that is heaven.

DELAYING

Part of the difficulty comes from the mindset of a fast-paced technological and information-driven age: we get what we want the way we want it right away. To work for something extremely distant and delayed is not always an attractive idea, because we like instant gratification and instant results. Another aspect of the difficulty arises from the fact that it takes courage and patience to forgo some things we discern to be obstacles to charity and heaven. We are filled with natural desires, and in satisfying these desires we may enjoy immense pleasure. In itself, satisfying natural desires is not necessarily bad, but it can be harmful in excess or out of appropriate context. Our appetites are good and for our good: for example, we desire sexual union because it unites man and woman into a loving communion and brings forth life. Yet simply because we want something does not mean we should have it, at least not whenever we want. Animals act on every impulse; rational minds can restrain these impulses in view of the broader picture of a well-lived life. Reason guides us in the discernment of when and how much of a good thing to take or forgo. It will often be easier to do what we want rather than to do what we ought when the two differ. Living for heaven means imitating God, who is all good and totally generous. Our deepened awareness of our sinfulness tells us that God is not always easy to imitate!

One final objection may be that, as we understand heaven in terms of happiness, we might claim longing for heaven is in itself selfish. We are, after all, hoping for our own good and happiness. However, it is in this very act of longing that our own will unites with God's will. God's greatest desire, we discover here, is the same as ours: that we live in perfect eternal communion and thereby experience surpassing joy. While the pursuit of our own happiness drives us, the true attainment thereof comes through the life of selfless love—charity—in imitation of Jesus Christ. Christ came to do the will of the Father, and so when we imitate Christ, we do the same in a manner that leads us along the way of salvation that he established for us.[2] Such imitation is therefore the best and most perfect of all pursuits, and is indeed our very purpose. Longing for heaven and living for it is the same as being true to our most authentic selves, to all of creation, and to God.

FOCUS FOR THE DAY'S PRAYER

Watch carefully for the moments of joy and happiness today, and keep them close. Notice they each are passing, they end, but they bring with them a smile of the soul. Try, in concert with the meditation, to imagine a day, or even a life, where only the good happens and where only joy abounds. Note that every joy and every good you encounter this day is potentially a foretaste of heaven, if you allow it to be so. Return to the fruits of this meditation throughout the day and ask the Lord to plant deep in your heart a right and holy longing for the joy that never fades: heaven.

Loving God, I turn my gaze to heaven and beg you to deepen my longing for that everlasting communion with you and all of your creation. Deepen my distaste for every impediment, every selfishness, and whatever may stand in my way. Strengthen me in all the virtues that I may clearly see the good and do it quickly, that I may thereby avoid anything that stands between you and me. Grant me knowledge of the true happiness to which you call me, and help me to pursue it with all my strength and in great patience and courage. By faith, hope, and love, draw me to yourself, oh Lover of my soul! Amen.

The Election and Choice of Heaven

I turn my heart and my soul toward you, O
wondrous heaven, everlasting glory, and endless
happiness, and choose my abiding place forever
within your beauteous and sacred mansions
and among your holy, longed-for tabernacles.[1]

Place yourself in the presence of God.
Ask him to inspire you.

In the book of Revelation, especially chapters 4 through 7, we
encounter images of the heavenly worship, of angels, saints, and
all creatures praising God before his throne. For good reason,
we speak of the Mass here on earth as an encounter with heaven,
the place where heaven and earth meet. In the Mass, just before

the Eucharistic Prayer, the priest recites or chants the preface: "And so, with Angels and Archangels, with Thrones and Dominions, and with all the hosts and Powers of heaven, we sing the hymn of your glory, as without end we acclaim," and then we join with the whole Church, heaven and earth, in a single song: "Holy, holy, holy, Lord God of Hosts!"

SPIRITUAL CREATURES— ANGELS AND DEMONS

As with so many of the other topics we have considered, angels tend to fall into a category the world considers quaint, novelties of the Church's imagination or outdated figures of a pre-scientific past. We cannot fail to recognize just how real the whole spiritual realm truly is or none of our meditations on heaven and hell have any footing. Perhaps the greatest proof we might encounter, aside from our own experiences of grace, is one from a rite of the Church: the Rite of Exorcism. Here we are before yet another controversial and often dismissed aspect of Church life.

In the middle of the Rite of Exorcism, the exorcist recites the Sanctus, the Holy, Holy, Holy, the same refrain we chant at Mass. Typically, this invocation causes an immediate and telling response from the demon: it begins to writhe, curse, and scream. It does so because those words are the words of the angels before the throne of God, a hymn the demon, a spiritual being, was originally created to chant with the whole heavenly host. By its choice to reject God and follow Satan, it will never chant those words again; these words stir up a hateful memory of its own corrupted purpose and the resulting eternal exclusion from heaven.

As heavy as that is, it is quite real. It gives profound proof of the reality of both angels and demons. As angels and demons are real, so are their eternal dwelling places in heaven and hell. Real, also, are their efforts to either aid us on or divert us from our journey to God.

On angels, the *Catechism* tells us that "the whole life of the Church benefits from the mysterious and powerful help of angels" (*CCC*, 334). "From its beginning until death human life is surrounded by their watchful care and intercession. 'Beside each believer stands an angel as protector and shepherd leading him to life' [St. Basil]. Already here on earth the Christian life shares by faith in the blessed company of angels and men united in God" (*CCC*, 336).

We are not alone in our pursuit of heaven. Each member of the Church on earth benefits from the prayerful and spiritual assistance of those in heaven because of the shared longing for eternal communion. We receive the assistance of angels and the intercession of the saints because God wants to give us every help possible to bring us into his eternal fold. As we have already said, he has given us everything we could possibly need to make our dreams and his longing an eternal reality. We must simply put our freedom to good use. We thus arrive at the topic of our next meditation.

"ELECTION—I CHOOSE . . ."

This and the following meditation differ from the previous ones. The previous topics invited a progressively intentional reflection upon purpose and destiny. The final two meditations aim at facilitating a personal choice, one built upon and resulting from the prayerful contemplation of all of the previous meditations' contents. As such, the remaining two meditations do not conclude with a Focus for the Day's Prayer section. Rather, they culminate in a formal decision after a dramatic consideration of all that is truly at stake.

De Sales again invokes the imagination. Imagine you are in an open field. You are kneeling in prayer. Standing before you is an angel, one you have never seen but you know quite well. It is your own guardian angel, the angel assigned to your protection, accompaniment, and care by God himself.

The angel unfolds a vision before you. You look upward, and you gaze upon the sky pierced and the heavens opened. You see in full detail all of the imagery you considered during the previous meditation and so much more: you behold everything of the heavenly reality. You see the throne of God with the entire heavenly host, and you hear the song of triumphant and glorious rejoicing. At the same moment, below you, hell opens to your gaze. There, you see all the torments and hear all of the despair and wailing you considered in your meditation on the subject, and much worse.

As you kneel in prayer before your angel, you are stricken by the power of what you have considered over and over again:

your freedom. In this culminating moment, you realize the whole truth and its powerful weight: you stand between heaven and hell. Each is open to you, wide open, and willing to receive you. You have the ability to choose, and you make the choice here, in this life. In making this grand choice of an eternity, you choose along with it the type of life and the earthly habits that facilitate the pursuit of your chosen eternity. You realize, with all certainty now, that the choice you make here in time determines your ultimate goal in life and this choice will stretch out unto all eternity the moment your soul leaves your body.

LORD OF ALL CREATION

In the vision you see heaven and hell as two opposites and both as viable possibilities. You also see, seated on the throne, God Almighty, Three-in-One, the Lord of all creation. Your gaze rises to God and rests there. His presence exerts a powerful draw over the whole of creation, a certain pulsation felt at the core of your being that, you notice, also pulls at every other creature in existence. Then Jesus Christ, Just and Merciful Judge, steps forth. As he does, you behold his Sacred Heart enkindled with flames. In the gentlest and most striking of ways, you discover that his heart is consumed with love for you. In this great moment, he opens his heart to you, a heart that was opened, pierced, in his death on the Cross. You know—with every physical and spiritual sense given you by God—just how much he loves you. The weight of such knowledge is awesome; your own tiny heart cannot contain the power and depth and breadth of that love. You weep.

You weep because you behold Christ glorified. As you do, you discover he still bears the marks of his Crucifixion. The light of heaven shines forth through the holes in his hands and feet. You know, pierced by this truth, that he suffered for love of you.

You see the mighty authority of the Judge, and you know his mercy and his justice. As you gaze into his eyes, you see the look he must have given to Mary Magdalene, to John and to Peter, and to all his followers, as much as to Pilate and Judas. By his look he invites you, even begs you, to come to him. He longs for you to be with him forever, and in his gaze you see the whole supremacy of God and the joy of eternity calling out to you. Look deeply, in prayer, into those eyes. Let him speak this longing into your soul. He begs you to choose heaven: "I have prepared a place for you in the heavenly city. Come, the way is simple."

Your guardian angel also looks at you and implores you, offering you in God's name every divine assistance in heaven and on earth to help you along that way. As you look on, Christ moves his right hand in beckoning and, resplendent in all the glory of heaven, the Blessed Virgin Mary comes forth. She looks at you, in tender and powerful motherhood, and smiles. Then, with all the love of a perfect mother, she takes your face in her hands and implores you: "Do not spurn the goodwill of God Almighty—nothing will ever cause you such sadness and despair! I, your heavenly Mother, have been and always will be constantly at work imploring God the Father on your behalf. I beg him perpetually to grant you every good gift from on high to strengthen you against all attack and all despair. Look to my Son, and say with me '*Fiat mihi secundum verbum tuum*—May it be done to me according to your word'" (see Lk 1:38).

Suddenly, behind the vision of God and the Blessed Virgin Mary, all of the inhabitants of the heavenly Jerusalem become visible. They turn their faces toward you. The vastness is overwhelming, countless are the thousands upon thousands. You recognize some of them, yet you feel as though you know all of them. In this moment, the whole of heaven looks to you with longing. They long to add one more voice to the chorus of praise before God's glory.

Suddenly, it strikes at your core: you matter. It feels as if an eternity has unfolded since you began. Recall the second mediation, during which you considered the fact that God does not need you, that God can get by just fine without you. It pierces your soul now with fresh insight. He does not need you—rather than need you, God *longs for you*. All at once, you now experience with the gaze of heaven upon you, the true weight of your importance. You are a beloved creature of God, loved into being by a God who is Love, created in God's image and likeness. You are personally, uniquely, lovingly called to share God's life and blessings.

As you see that glorious place before your own eyes, your soul stirs for its homeland. You discover the whole heavenly host and all the blessed long to have you in their company. You are not lost in a sea of millions; you are a singularly precious jewel of God's creation, a jewel made to shine uniquely with the glory of God.

You take a deep breath, stumbling to embrace the vastness of what you have beheld and the simplicity of what lies before you. You close your eyes for a brief moment to regain your bearing. You realize your perception of reality has been altered forever. Having seen what you have seen, you now understand that these eternal realities lie just beneath the surface of the visible world, just beneath the surface of every choice and every decision. As you open your eyes again, heaven and hell are less visible, but you know them to be there . . . and both to be possible.

"I Choose."

Hell, I detest you now and forever more.
I detest your torments and your pains.
I detest your accursed and wretched eternity.
Above all, I detest the eternal blasphemies
    And maledictions that you eternally vomit forth
        against my God.

I turn my heart and my soul toward you, O wondrous
    heaven,
Everlasting glory, and endless happiness,
And choose my abiding place forever within your

Beauteous and sacred mansions
  And among your holy, longed-for tabernacles.

O my God, I bless your mercy and I accept
The offer you are pleased to give to me.
O Jesus, my Savior, I accept your everlasting love
And I hail the place and lodging you have purchased
  for me in this blessed Jerusalem.
  Beyond any other reason I do so in order to love
    and bless you forever and ever. [2]

Blessed Mary, my dearest Mother and Queen,
My guardian angel, all the saints to whom I have
  entrusted
My life by name or devotion,
I accept your companionship
And the grace of your prayerful intercession.
Please pray for me now and be at my side always,
That I may take to this lovely road,
Through trial and grace,
And live each moment
With heaven as my aim.
Amen.

The Election and Choice the Soul Makes of a Devout Life

I turn to you, my own Jesus, King of
happiness and eternal glory, and I embrace
you with all the strength of my soul. I
adore you with my whole heart. I choose
you to be my King now and forever.[1]

*Place yourself in the presence of God.
Ask him to inspire you.*

The ninth meditation's purpose was to prompt a concrete choice
between eternities. The present and final one is similar in its

scope and will conclude once more with a resolution. Here, the choice will be between earthly ways, temporal realities: the here and now. This present decision relies upon the previous one; it represents the choice to live day-to-day in practical pursuit of heaven, now formally chosen as the ultimate goal. Again, de Sales has recourse to the imaginative faculty to awaken a resolve to live intentionally in view of that ultimate goal.

Imagine once more that you are in a field, attended by your guardian angel. Heaven above and hell below are no longer visible; the consideration shifts to the present, to this life. Rather than above and below, you look to the left and to the right. You behold two kingdoms, realms completely commingled within the temporal order. Before your eyes, their members—all the living men and women on the face of the earth—separate perfectly, one from the other. As you look on, God gives you his particular insight to see past exteriors and into the very heart of every human person. What normally hides in the sanctuary of the soul is now manifest for all to see.

THE KINGDOM OF SIN

To the left, you see the devil. He sits on a massive, gnarled throne, surrounded by demons and evil spirits. Thousands upon thousands of attendants flank the demons, men and women of every background, age, and ethnicity. They pay homage to their king and lord by all types of sins, knowing that these illicit thoughts, words, and deeds please him. Each face is marked differently: some with rage or anger, others with anxiety and worry, still others frenzied with passion and lust. Some relish their sins more than others do, but some combination of pride, covetousness, lust, anger, envy, sloth, or gluttony adorns every face. Over the entire kingdom hovers a general contentment in the shared commitment to honor this king. Some flaunt their sins extravagantly, others act with less flair or confidence.

As you look on, it gradually becomes clear that the principal commonality among all the subjects is little more than their commitment to sin. Whether near or far from the throne, a subtle hum of dismay resonates. As you watch, what once appeared to be a unity quickly dissipates.

You slowly notice that division in fact characterizes the whole kingdom. Each man or woman clamors for praise and recognition from the king and from one another. In pride, they all seek to distinguish themselves from each other. They press and claw against one another in pursuit of honor and in hope of power. They use each other, seeking their own advantage; curses and insults linger eerily. Everyone is desperately subject to his or her passions and viscous pride. Any show of apparent love or generosity is unveiled; each longs separately for power and praise.

As you look on, marvel at the fact that these are the living men and women of the world. Living still in the flesh, their eternity has not yet been decided. These men and women are created, like you, in the image and likeness of God. They are the ones ensnared by lies, those who have rejected the gifts of grace held out to them by their Father. As you look, your heart is rent, not with terror but with urgent compassion.

THE KINGDOM OF LOVE

This sentiment draws your heart and your gaze toward the other kingdom to the right. At its center you see Christ crucified and glorious, and again you see his Sacred Heart. You notice a greater familiarity than you knew in the last vision; now, your heart somehow beats with his. You feel his burning compassion for all of humanity, especially for those who are lost. He smiles as you understand this, and you sense your heart is turned with his toward those who are lost but not without hope.

You are deeply aware that Christ is constantly working to break through the grime that covers the hearts of sinners, trying to stir up in them a true awareness of their real purpose. You see him holding a shepherd's staff, and you know a deep peace. You smile, understanding the Shepherd's heart. You burn with the desire to help.

As your focus broadens, you notice the inhabitants of this kingdom. As you take in the broad landscape of this kingdom, its appearance surprises you. Only now do you realize the other kingdom was dark and you had failed to notice that darkness until you knew the Light. Now, gazing over the whole vastness of the devout souls of the earth, your senses are elevated as you notice the hum of dismay gives way to the gentle song of devotion and virtue.

Men and women from every walk of life are present before your gaze. Many are helping others, holding up the disabled or speaking patiently to the elderly. Laughter reigns, and an air of peace lingers. As you look on, more details come into focus. You see the weakness and struggle of many of them, their sacrifices and sufferings and sadnesses. Where in the other kingdom these were exploited by neighbors, now those nearest reach out to comfort, to help, and to share.

All at once, it becomes clear to you. Where the other kingdom was divided neighbor against neighbor, here every man and woman is for God. Where division ruled there, the unity here is charity. Where there was anxious despair before, here there is steady hope. The members of this kingdom share a common aim: to love God and one another. You notice they all wait on the Lord. They lift up their hearts to God, looking as constantly to him as possible in the midst of faithfulness to their worldly obligations, to work and health and family and friendships.

God is the criterion of their choices and the clear goal of their actions. You notice that, while nothing here is perfect, perfection is their aim. Their lives, albeit in varying degrees, are lived in imitation of Christ.

From just beneath the surface, *glory emanates*.

———

In a real way, you know you have already turned from Satan and his kingdom of sin by the good fruits of these meditations. This should bring you a certain relief. However, you also know you have not yet fully committed yourself to the kingdom of Love. Somehow, as you looked over that place, you knew yourself still an onlooker, inspired and at peace but slightly taken aback by the goodwill of the members of that place.

Recall in your heart the power of forgiveness, the grace to have sin washed away and be strengthened against its return. See once again the whole heavenly host gazing upon you, with Christ and his Mother at the fore, beckoning, waiting. You know your eternal destiny. The time has come to be finished meditating and begin living.

The choice you made in the last meditation is put into practice here and now, day by day. It was not a once-and-for-all choice because your nature remains sinful and because the kingdom that opposes God longs for your presence as much as does God's kingdom. The broad choice for heaven is the horizon choice, and one you put into practice each and every time you freely make decisions, each and every single day of your life. Therefore, one more major decision remains.

The final fruit of the meditations is to commit to a way of life, what de Sales calls "the devout life." It is a choice that must be renewed, refreshed, and reinvigorated daily, for it is the decision to bring that ultimate goal off the horizon and into all of your daily movements and activities. Understanding heaven and considering it constantly throughout daily life is the fundamental and greatest fruit of these meditations.

De Sales had an expression for living the devout life. A life that entails working daily to live out faithfulness to the commandment to love God above all else and love your neighbor as yourself is truly a life of striving to live like Jesus Christ. In a rather simple manner, de Sales summarized the whole of the devout life with a simple exhortation: "Live, Jesus!" It can be taken to mean both, "Let Jesus live in me!" and, "May I live a life like his!"

The final moment of this meditation is a moment of conversion. Conversion is always a "turning away from" as much as a "turning toward." So now, turn finally, completely, to God. Lift up your heart! Leave behind your former ways. Refreshed by grace with trust and great confidence in God, you must now make the choice to set out on the pathway of charity filled with ardent faith and joy-filled hope.

"ELECTION"

Say finally, with St. Francis de Sales and all who have walked this way:

> O world! O abominable troop!
> No, never shall you see me beneath your banner!
> I have forever abandoned your mad, fruitless ways.
> King of pride, accursed king, infernal spirit,
> I renounce you and all your empty pomps!
> I detest you and all your works.

I turn to you, my own Jesus,
King of happiness and eternal glory,
And I embrace you with all the strength of my soul.
I adore you with my whole heart.
I choose you to be my King now and forever.
By this inviolable act of fidelity
I pay you irrevocable homage.
  I submit myself to your holy laws and ordinances.

O holy Virgin, my beloved Lady,
I choose you for my guide.
I put myself under your direction and
  Offer you particular respect and special reverence.

My guardian angel, present me to this sacred assembly.
Do not forsake me until I have been enrolled
In this blessed company.
With them I say and I will say
Forever in testimony to my choice:
"Live, Jesus! Live, Jesus!"[2]
Amen.

Conclusion

Perhaps I could have been more forthright at the beginning. There, I might have told you that you would finish this little set of reflections and realize something very important: instead of ending, something has only just begun. I might have told you this is really just the beginning of what St. Francis de Sales calls an ***Introduction*** *to the Devout Life*.

I might have told you that, when you finish praying through all of these meditations, you will find yourself standing with one foot on a path. You will have just decided between two final destinations, and you will have just chosen to take this path, a path that leads through the field of life, upward and into the horizon. Certainly not the easiest path to take, it is also not too difficult. It leads to the narrow gate Jesus spoke of in Matthew 7:14. Through that gate, the Son shines eternally. If you have prayed through all of these meditations, you now see quite clearly that you have only just begun.

I could have told you all of that, I suppose, at the outset, but I believe it would not have meant much then. I can say it now because I know you understand what I mean when I say this: welcome to the adventure of the rest of your life.

————

I conclude with some encouragement. Near the end of his book, de Sales includes a second set of meditations to be made annually in renewing the commitment to living the devout life. He pointedly calls you to exclaim, "O my soul, you are made for God! Woe to you if you are satisfied with anything less than God!" Lingering with that fact, he invites you to, "raise your soul aloft on this consideration. Remind it that it is eternal and worthy of eternity. Fill it with courage for this project."[1] He could not have put it better. This indeed is a project, a most worthy endeavor, and one you have just chosen to undertake: to live for heaven in the day-to-day details of your entire life.

Know that you undertake this project of faith in great company. Countless men and women have gone before you and have been generous enough to record their own thoughts, suggestions, and encouragements. They are the saints; our Catholic library is full of some two thousand years of their writings, all meant to assist you here and now. Know that you make this journey at present with millions of others and the world is full of millions more who deep in their hearts long to set out as well. Many of them have not yet realized the path exists. Know finally that you make this journey of faith in the context of the Catholic Church, which Christ instituted himself to make sure that, when this day would come, you would have everything you need and more to journey, and journey well. He did this . . . all for you. If you feel spoiled by God, if you blush at the awesomeness of this tender care of his, you are finally beginning to understand.

Along the way, you may find it helpful to return to these meditations to refresh your commitment to the choices you have made. You may also find it helpful to do them in the exact manner laid out by our great guide, St. Francis de Sales. You will quite likely find the rest of his book not really an introduction but rather a spiritual compendium, quite helpful as well. My hope and my prayer here is to simply help you in getting started on this tremendous, wild, and beautiful adventure that is the journey into the splendid love of God.

As I complete this book, I do so with a prayer for all who will one day read it. The Lord has, in his mysterious and tender way, drawn us together for a portion of the journey. Let us take confidence in the fact that together we have joined so gentle and good a spiritual master as St. Francis de Sales. Together with him, let us smile, lift up our hearts, and say, "Live, Jesus!"

Acknowledgments

I am humbly indebted to so many who helped make this little work of prayer into what it has become. First and foremost, I owe thanks to God and then to my amazing family for the innumerable gifts and blessings that we share. I am also grateful to St. Francis de Sales Seminary, the faculty of which gave me my first copy of *Introduction to the Devout Life*. I gratefully acknowledge that without the help of Robert Feind, Brandon and Elissa Bowlin, Danny and Julie Catanese, and Fr. Wally Stohrer, S.J., this book would never have made it beyond my journal. I thank my mother, Peggy Burns, as well as Carrie Froelich for their keen eyes and skillful editing; Lisa Rehlinger for her cheerful help; as well as Kristi McDonald and the staff of Ave Maria Press for all the finishing touches. And finally, I owe more thanks than I could ever articulate to Fr. Luke Strand and Sr. Lily Marie, whose encouragement and invaluable friendship nudged me forward the whole way through.

St. Francis de Sales's Original Meditations[1]

THE FIRST MEDITATION— ON OUR CREATION

PREPARATION

1. Place yourself in the presence of God.

2. Beseech him to inspire you.

CONSIDERATIONS

1. Consider that a certain number of years ago you were not yet in the world and that your present being was truly nothing. My soul, where were we at that time? The world had already existed for a long time, but of us there was as yet nothing.

2. God has drawn you out of that nothingness to make you what you now are and he has done so solely out of his own goodness and without need of you.

3. Consider the nature God has given to you. It is the highest in this visible world; it is capable of eternal life and of being perfectly united to his Divine Majesty.

AFFECTIONS AND RESOLUTIONS

1. Humble yourself profoundly before God, and like the Psalmist say with all your heart: "Lord, before you I am truly nothing. How were you mindful of me so as to create me?" Alas, my soul, you were engulfed in that ancient nothing and you would still be there if God had not drawn you out of it. What could you have done in that nothingness?

2. Return thanks to God. My great and good Creator, how great is my debt to you since you were moved to draw me out of nothing and by your mercy to make me what I am! What can I ever do to bless your holy name in a worthy manner and to render thanks to your immense mercy?

3. Rebuke yourself. Alas, my Creator, instead of uniting myself to you in love and service I have become a total rebel by my disorderly affections, separated myself from you, strayed far from you in order to embrace sin, and shown no more honor to your goodness than if you were not my Creator.

4. Abase yourself before God. My soul, "know that the Lord is your God. He has made you, and you have not made yourself." O God, I am "the work of your hands."

5. From now on, then, I will no longer be self-complacent, since of myself I am nothing. O dust and ashes, or rather you who are truly nothing, why do you glory in yourself? To humble myself I resolve to do such and such things, to suffer such and such humiliations. I desire to change my life and henceforward to follow my Creator and to find honor in the state of being he has given me, employing it entirely in obedience to his will by such means as will be taught me and about which I will ask my spiritual director.

CONCLUSION

1. Give thanks to God. "Bless your God, O my soul, and let all my being praise his holy name," for his goodness has drawn me out of nothing and his mercy has created me.

2. Offer. O my God, with all my heart I offer you the being you have given me. I dedicate and consecrate it to you.

3. Pray. O God, strengthen me in these affections and resolutions. O Holy Virgin, recommend them to the mercy of your Son together with all those for whom I am bound to pray; and so on.

    Our Father, Hail Mary.

After completing your prayer go back over it for a moment and out of the considerations you have made gather a little devotional bouquet to refresh you during the rest of the day.

THE SECOND MEDITATION—ON THE END FOR WHICH WE WERE CREATED

PREPARATION

1. Place yourself in the presence of God.

2. Beseech him to inspire you.

CONSIDERATIONS

1. God has placed you in this world not because he needs you in any way—you are altogether useless to him—but only to exercise his goodness in you by giving you his grace and glory. For this purpose he has given you intellect to know him, memory to be mindful of him, will to love him, imagination to picture to yourself his benefits, eyes to see his wonderful works, tongue to praise him, and so on with the other faculties.

2. Since you have been placed in this world for this purpose, all actions contrary to it must be rejected and avoided and those not serving this end should be despised as empty and useless.

3. Consider the unhappiness of worldly people who never think of all this but live as if they believe themselves created only to build houses, plant trees, pile up wealth, and do frivolous things.

AFFECTIONS AND RESOLUTIONS

1. Humble yourself and rebuke your soul for its misery, which up to now has been so great that it has seldom or never reflected on all this. Alas, you will say, what did I think about, O my God, when I did not think of you? What did I remember when I forgot you? What did I love when I did not love you? Alas, I should have fed upon the truth but I glutted myself with vanity and served the world which was made only to serve me.

2. Detest your past life. Vain thoughts and useless plans, I renounce you. Hateful and foolish memories, I abjure you. False and treacherous friendships, wasted, wretched deeds, useless self-indulgence, and onerous pleasures, I reject you.

3. Turn to God. My God and my Savior, you shall hence-forward be the sole object of my thoughts. I will no longer turn my mind to thoughts that displease you. Every day of my life my memory will be filled with your great mercy that has been so sweetly shown to me. You shall be the joy of my heart and the sweetness of my affections. The trifling, foolish things which I have hitherto devoted myself

to, the vain uses to which I have put my days, and the affections that have filled my heart shall from now on be looked on with horror. For this intention I will use such and such remedies.

CONCLUSION

1. Thank God, who has made you for so exalted an end. Lord, you have made me to the end that I forever may enjoy your immeasurable glory. When shall I be worthy of it, when shall I bless you as I ought?

2. Offer. My beloved Creator, I offer you these affections and resolutions with all my heart and soul.

3. Pray. I beseech you, O God, to look with favor on my desires and purposes and give your holy blessing to my soul to the end that it may be able to accomplish them through the merits of the Blood your blessed Son shed upon the Cross, etc.

    Make a little spiritual bouquet.

THE THIRD MEDITATION— ON GOD'S BENEFACTIONS

PREPARATION

1. Place yourself in the presence of God.

2. Beseech him to inspire you.

CONSIDERATIONS

1. Consider the corporeal benefits that God has bestowed on you: the body itself, goods provided for its maintenance, health, lawful comforts, friends, aids, and helps. Consider all this in contrast to so many other persons more deserving than yourself but destitute of such blessings. Some are disabled in body, health, or members; others are left helpless under opprobrium, insult, and infamy. Still others are ground down by poverty. God has not decreed that you be so miserable.

2. Consider your gifts of mind. How many men there are in the world who are dull of mind, mad, or insane. Why are not you among their number? It is because God has favored you. How many there are who have been brought up harshly and in gross ignorance while God's providence has brought you up in freedom and dignity!

3. Consider your spiritual favors. Philothea, you are a child of the Church. From your childhood God has taught you to know him. How often he has given his sacraments to you! How often you have received his inspirations, interior lights, and admonitions for your amendment! How often he has forgiven your faults! How often has he delivered you from those occasions of damnation to which you have been exposed! Were not all those past years a time of leisure and opportunity to improve your soul's good? By

noting each particular thing you perceive in some small way how gentle and gracious God has been to you.

AFFECTIONS AND RESOLUTIONS

1. Marvel at God's goodness. How good my God has been in my behalf! How good indeed! Lord, how rich is your heart in mercy and how generous in good will! My soul, let us always recall the many graces he has shown to us.

2. Marvel at your own ingratitude. What am I, O Lord, that you are mindful of me? And how great is my unworthiness! Alas, I have trodden your blessings underfoot. I have abused your graces and have perverted them into dishonor and contempt of your sovereign goodness. I have opposed the depths of my ingratitude to the depths of your grace and favor.

3. Arouse yourself to make this acknowledgement. Up, then, O my heart, resolve to be no longer faithless, ungrateful, and disloyal to this great benefactor. And how "shall my soul be henceforth wholly subject to God" who has wrought so many wonders and graces in me and for me?

4. Philothea, keep your body safe from such and such pleasures and consecrate it to the service of God who has done so much for it. Set your soul to know and acknowledge him by such exercises as are needed for that purpose. Use diligently all the Church's means to save yourself and to love God. Yes, O my God, I will be assiduous in prayer

and at the sacraments. I will listen to your holy word and put your inspirations and counsels into practice.

CONCLUSION

1. Thank God for the knowledge he has now given you of your duties and for all benefits already received.

2. Offer him your heart together with all your resolutions.

3. Pray that he may give you strength to practice them faithfully through the merits of his Son's death. Implore the intercession of the Virgin and the saints.

   Our Father, etc.

   Make a little spiritual bouquet.

THE FOURTH MEDITATION—ON SIN

PREPARATION

1. Place yourself in the presence of God.

2. Beseech him to inspire you.

CONSIDERATIONS

1. Recall to mind how long it is since you began to sin and note how greatly sins have multiplied in your heart since that first beginning and how every day you have increased them against God, yourself, and your neighbor by deed, word, desire, and thought.

2. Consider your evil inclinations and how often you have
    given way to them. By these two points you will discover
    that your sins are more numerous than the hairs of your
    head, yes, more than the sands of the sea.

3. Consider particularly the sin of the ingratitude to God, a
    general sin that reaches out to all the rest and makes them
    infinitely more enormous. Note then how many benefits
    God has granted you and how you have misused all of
    them against their giver. Note especially how many of
    his inspirations you have despised and how many good
    movements you have rendered useless. Even more than all
    the rest remember how many times you have received the
    sacraments—and where are their fruits? What has become
    of those precious jewels with which your beloved Spouse
    adorned you? All of them have been buried beneath your
    iniquities. With what preparations did you receive them?
    Think about such ingratitude. So often God has run after
    you to save you, and you have always fled before him in
    order to destroy yourself.

AFFECTIONS AND RESOLUTIONS

1. Be in the utmost consternation at your misery. O my
    God! do I dare to stand before your eyes?
         Alas, I am only the corruption of the world and a
    sink of ingratitude and iniquity. Is it possible that I have
    been faithless that I have left neither a single sense nor
    one of my mental faculties uncorrupted, unviolated, and

undefiled, and that not so much as a single day of my life has passed when I have not done most evil deeds? Should I thus repay the benefits brought to me by my Creator and by my Redeemer's Blood?

2. As pardon and, like the prodigal son, like Magdalen, like a woman who has defiled her marriage bed with adulterous deeds of every kind, cast yourself at the feet of the Lord. Have mercy, Lord, upon this sinful creature. Alas, O living fountain of compassion, have pity on this miserable wretch.

3. Resolve to live a better life. No, Lord, nevermore, with the help of your grace, no, nevermore will I abandon myself to sin. Alas, I have loved it too much. I detest it and I embrace you, the Father of mercy. In you I wish to live and die.

4. To wipe out my past sins I will bravely accuse myself of them, and I will not leave one of them without driving it out.

5. I will do all that I can to root out completely what is planted in my heart, particularly such and such things that have most troubled me.

6. To do this I will unfailingly embrace the means that I have been counselled to adopt, knowing that I have never done enough to repair such grievous faults.

CONCLUSION

1. Return thanks to God who has waited for you until this hour and has given you these good affections.

2. Offer your heart to him so that you can put them into effect.

3. Pray that he will strengthen you, etc.

THE FIFTH MEDITATION—ON DEATH

PREPARATION

1. Place yourself in the presence of God.

2. Beg him for his grace.

3. Imagine yourself to be lying on your deathbed, extremely ill and without any hope of recovery.

CONSIDERATIONS

1. Consider how uncertain is the day of your death. My soul, one day you will leave this body. When will it be? In winter or in summer? In the city or in the country? By day or at night? Suddenly or after due preparation? From sickness or by accident? Will you have time to make your confession or not? Will you be assisted by your confessor and spiritual director? Unfortunately, we know nothing whatsoever about all this. Only one thing is certain: we will die and sooner than we think.

2. Consider that for you the world will then come to an end because for you it will no longer be. Before your eyes it will be hurled over and over. Yes, at that moment all the pleasure, frivolity, worldly joy, and useless affection will appear before you like phantoms and misty clouds. Ah, my wretched soul, for what toys and idle fancies have I offended God! You will see that you have forsaken him for nothing at all. On the contrary, devotion and good works will then seem sweet and desirable. Why did I not follow that lovely pleasant path? Sins that once seemed so small will then appear as huge as mountains but your devotion very little.

3. Consider the long, languishing goodbye that your soul will give to this base world. It will bid farewell to wealth, to empty things and useless associations, to pleasures and pastimes, to friends and neighbors, to parents, children, husband, wife, in a word, to every creature, and at last to its own body, which it will leave behind, pale, ghastly, wasted, hideous, and loathsome.

4. Consider with what haste they will carry away that body and bury it in the earth, and this done, the world will scarcely think about you or keep your memory, any more than you have thought of others. "May God grant him peace," they will say, and that is all. O Death, how powerful thou art! How pitiless thou art!

5. Consider how the soul after leaving the body goes its way, either to the right or to the left. Alas, where will your soul go? Which way will it take? It will be none other than the one begun in this world.

AFFECTIONS AND RESOLUTIONS

1. Pray to God and cast yourself into his arms. Lord, take me under your protection on that dreadful day. Only make that last hour happy and favorable to me and rather let all the other days of my life be sad and sorrowful.

2. Despise this world. O world, since I do not know the hour when I must leave you, I will no longer set my heart on you. My dear friends, my dear relations, let me no longer love you except with a holy friendship that can last eternally. Why should I unite myself to you in such wise as to be forced to give up and break our union?

3. I wish to prepare myself for that hour and to take all needed care to make a blessed departure. With all my power I wish to insure a proper state of conscience and to correct such and such defects.

CONCLUSION

1. Return thanks to God for these resolutions which he has given you. Offer them to his Majesty. Beseech him again to grant you a happy death through the merits of his Son's

death. Implore the assistance of the Virgin Mary and the saints.

2. Our Father, Hail Mary.

3. Make a bouquet of myrrh.

THE SIXTH MEDITATION—ON JUDGMENT

PREPARATION

1. Place yourself in the presence of God.

2. Beseech him to inspire you.

CONSIDERATIONS

1. At the end, after the time God has allotted for the duration of this world and after many signs and portents at which men will "wither away through fear" and apprehension, fire like a raging torrent will burn and reduce to ashes the whole face of the earth. Nothing that we see here will escape it.

2. After this deluge of flame and thunderbolts all men will rise from the earth except those who have already risen, and at the voice of the angel they will appear in the valley of Josaphat. But, alas, what differences there will be! Some will be glorious and resplendent in body others will appear in hideous, frightful bodies.

3. Consider the majesty with which the sovereign Judge will appear, surrounded by all the angels and saints. Before him will be borne his cross, shining more brilliantly than the sun, a standard of mercy to the good and of punishment to the wicked.

4. By his awful command, which will be swiftly carried out, this sovereign Judge will separate the good from the bad and place the one at his right hand and the other at his left. It will be an everlasting separation and after it these two groups will never again be together.

5. When this separation has been made and all consciences laid bare we will clearly see the malice of the wicked and the contempt they have shown for God, and we will also see the repentance of the good and the effect of the graces they received from God. Nothing will lie hidden. O God, what horror for the evil, what comfort for the good!

6. Consider that last sentence passed on the wicked: "Depart from me, you cursed, into everlasting fire which was prepared for the devil and his companions." Weigh well those heavy words. "Depart," he says. It is a word of eternal abandonment that God utters to those unhappy souls and by it he banishes them forever from his face. He calls them cursed. O my soul, what a curse, what a general curse this is since it includes every kind of evil! It is an irrevocable curse for it includes both time and eternity. He adds, "into everlasting fire." Behold, O my heart, that

vast eternity! O eternal eternity of pain how dreadful thou art!

7. Consider the contrary sentence passed on the good. "Come," says the Judge. Ah this is the sweet word of salvation by which God draws us to himself and receives us into the bosom of his goodness. "You blessed of my Father." O welcome blessing, which includes all blessings! "Possess the kingdom prepared for you from the foundation of the world." O God, what a grace this is, for this kingdom shall never have an end!

AFFECTIONS AND RESOLUTIONS

1. Tremble, O my soul, at the remembrance of these things. O God, who can give me surety for that day when "the pillars of heaven" will tremble with fear?

2. Detest your sins for they alone can ruin you on that dreadful day.

3. Ah, I will judge myself now so that I may not be judged! I will examine my conscience and condemn, accuse, and amend myself so that the Judge will not condemn me on that dreadful day. I will confess my sins and accept all necessary advice, etc.

CONCLUSION

1. Thank God, who has given you means to safeguard yourself on that day and time to do penance.

2. Offer him your heart in order to do penance.

3. Our Father, Hail Mary.
    Prepare a bouquet.

THE SEVENTH MEDITATION—ON HELL

PREPARATION

1. Place yourself in the presence of God.

2. Humble yourself and ask his assistance.

3. Picture to yourself a gloomy city burning with Sulphur
    and foul-smelling pitch and filled with people who cannot
    escape from it.

CONSIDERATIONS

1. The damned are in the depths of hell as though trapped in
    a doomed city where they suffer unspeakable torments in
    every sense and every member. Just as they used all their
    senses and members to commit sin, so in every member
    and in every sense they endure the punishments due to
    sin. Because of base and evil looks the eyes will endure the
    horrid sight of devils and hell. Because they took delight
    in vicious conversations the ears will hear nothing but
    wailing, lamentation, and despairing cries. So too for the
    other senses.

2. Beyond all such torments there is one still greater—the privation and loss of God's glory from which they are forever barred. If Absalom found privation of the loving face of David, his father, more grievous than exile, O God, what grief it is to be forever concluded from the sight of your sweet and gracious countenance!

3. Most of all consider the eternity of these sufferings, for it alone makes hell unbearable. Alas, if a flea in our ear or the heat of a slight fever makes a brief night long and tedious, how terrible will be eternal night with all its torments! Out of this eternity are born eternal despair and infinite rage and blasphemy.

AFFECTIONS AND RESOLUTIONS

1. Strike terror into your soul by the words of Isaias: "O my soul, how can you dwell with this everlasting burning and in this devouring fire?" How can you think of parting from God forever?

2. Confess that you have deserved hell and at many times! But henceforth I will follow the contrary path. Why should I go down into that infinite pit?

3. I will make such and such efforts to avoid sin, for it alone can bring me to that eternal death.

   Give thanks; offer; pray.

THE EIGHTH MEDITATION—ON PARADISE

PREPARATION

1. Place yourself in the presence of God.

2. Make an invocation.

CONSIDERATIONS

1. Consider a calm, beautiful night and think how good it is to see the sky with its countless varied stars. Next add its beauty to that of a fine day in such wise that the brilliant sun does not prevent a clear view of the stars or moon. Then say boldly that all this beauty put together is of no value when compared to the excellence of God's paradise. Oh how lovely, how desirable is that place, how precious is that city!

2. Consider the nobility, beauty, and number of the citizens and inhabitants of that fortunate land—those millions upon millions of angels, cherubim, and seraphim, those bands of apostles, martyrs, confessors, virgins, and holy women. It is a countless throng. How fortunate is that company! If the least among them is more beautiful to see than the whole world, what will it be to see all of them together! O my God, how fortunate they are! They forever sing their sweet canticle of eternal love; they forever enjoy constant happiness. They give one another ineffable

contentment and live in the consolation of a happy an indissoluble union.

3. Finally, how good it is for them to consider God who forever favors them with his beloved presence and by it infuses into their hearts the deepest delights! How good it is to be united forever with the source of all good! They are like happy birds that fly and sing perpetually in that divine air which surrounds them on every side with incredible pleasures. There each one does his utmost and without envy sings his Creator's praise. Be blessed forever, O sweet and sovereign Creator and Savior, you who are so good to us and so generously share with us your glory! With an everlasting blessing God blesses all his saints. Be blessed forever, he says, my beloved creatures, for you have served me and you will praise me eternally with so great a love and zeal.

AFFECTIONS AND RESOLUTIONS

1. Marvel at this heavenly fatherland and praise it. How beautiful you are, my dear Jerusalem, and how happy are your inhabitants.

2. Reproach your heart for its lack of courage up to now and for straying far from the path to this glorious dwelling. Why have I wandered so far from my sovereign happiness? Wretch that I am, for trifling, bitter pleasures I have a thousand thousand times forsaken these eternal

and infinite delights. How could I think of despising
such deniable rewards for such empty and contemptible
desires?

3. Fervently aspire to this most delightful abode. My good
    and sovereign Lord, since it has pleased you to direct my
    steps into your ways, nevermore will I turn away from
    them. Let us go forward, my dear soul, to that infinite
    repose, let us travel on to that blessed land which is prom-
    ised to us. What are we doing in Egypt?

4. I will therefore put away everything that might lead me
    astray or delay me on this journey.

5. I will do such and such things as may conduct me thither.
        Give thanks; offer; pray.

THE NINTH MEDITATION—THE
ELECTION AND CHOICE OF HEAVEN

PREPARATION

1. Place yourself in the presence of God.

2. Humble yourself before him and pray that he may inspire
    you.

CONSIDERATIONS

Imagine yourself to be in an open field, alone with your guardian angel, like young Tobias on his way to Rages. Imagine that he shows high heaven open before you with all its joys as pictured in the meditation you have made, and that he then shows you hell lying open beneath you with all the torments described in the mediation on hell. Situated thus in imagination and kneeling before your guardian angel:

1. Consider that it is strictly true that you stand between heaven and hell and that each of them lies open to receive you according to the choice you make.

2. Consider that the choice of one or the other of them that we make in this world will last eternally in the world to come.

3. Also, that although each of them is open to receive you in keeping with your choice, yet God, who is prepared to give you hell by his justice or heaven by his mercy, desires with an incomparable desire that you choose heaven. With all his power your guardian angel also urges you to do this and in God's name offers you a thousand graces and a thousand helps to assist you to obtain it.

4. From the heights of heaven Jesus Christ mercifully looks down upon you and graciously invites you there. He says, "Come, dear soul, and find everlasting rest in my bountiful arms where I have prepared undying delight for you in

the abundance of my love." With your inward eyes behold
the Blessed Virgin who maternally bids you: "Courage,
my child, do not spurn my Son's desires or the many sighs
that I have cast forth for you as I yearn with him for your
eternal salvation." Behold the saints who exhort you and
the millions of blessed souls who sweetly invite you and
wish only to see your heart one day joined with theirs
in praising and loving God forever. They assure you that
the way to heaven is not as difficult as the world makes it
out to be. "Be of good heart, dear brother," they say. "He
who carefully considers the way of devotion by which we
ascended hither will see that we acquired these delights by
pleasures incomparably sweeter than those of the world."

ELECTION

1. Hell, I detest you now and forevermore. I detest your
    torments and your pains. I detest your accursed and
    wretched eternity. Above all, I detest the eternal blas-
    phemies and maledictions that you eternally vomit forth
    against my God. I turn my heart and my soul toward
    you, O wondrous heaven, everlasting glory, and endless
    happiness, and choose my abiding place forever within
    your beauteous and sacred mansions and among your
    holy, longed-for tabernacles. O my God, I bless your
    mercy and I accept the offer you are pleased to give to me.
    O Jesus, my Savior, I accept your everlasting love and I
    hail the place and lodging you have purchased for me in

this blessed Jerusalem. Beyond any other reason I do so in order to love and bless you forever and ever.

2. Accept the help that the Virgin and the saints offer you. Promise that you will press forward on your way to join them. Reach out your hand to your guardian angel so that he may lead you on. Encourage your soul to make this choice.

THE TENTH MEDITATION— THE ELECTION AND CHOICE THE SOUL MAKES OF A DEVOUT LIFE

PREPARATION

1. Place yourself in the presence of God.

2. Humble yourself before him and implore his help.

CONSIDERATIONS

1. Again imagine yourself to be in an open field along with your guardian angel and that you see the devil seated high upon a huge throne, attended by many infernal spirits and surrounded by a great throng of worldly people who with uncovered heads hail him as their lord and pay him homage, some by one sin and some by another. Note the faces of all the unfortunate courtiers of that abominable king. See how some of them are furious with hatred, envy, and

anger, others are consumed with care and burdened down by worries as they think and strive to heap up wealth. See how others are bent upon vain pursuits that bring empty and unsatisfying pleasure and how others are defiled, ruined, and putrefied by their brutish lusts. See how they are without rest, order, and decency. See how they despise one another and make only a false show of love. In a word, you see there a common wealth lying in ruins and tyrannized over by this accursed king. All this will move you to compassion.

2. On the right side you see Jesus Christ crucified. With heartfelt love he prays for these poor tormented people so that they may be set free from such tyranny, and he calls them to himself. Around him you see a great throng of devout souls together with their guardian angels. Contemplate the beauty of this devout kingdom. How beautiful it is to see this throng of virgins, both men and women, all whiter than lilies, and this gathering of widows filled with sacred mortification and humility! See the crowded ranks of the married who live so calmly together in mutual respect, which cannot be had without great charity. See how these devout souls wed care of the exterior house to that of the interior, that is, the love of their earthly spouse with that of the heavenly Spouse. Consider them all as a group and see how all of them in a holy, sweet, and lovely manner attend on our Lord, and how they long to place him in the center of their hearts. They are joyful, but with

a gracious, loving, and well-ordered joy. They love one another, but with a most pure and sacred love. Among these devout people those who suffer afflictions are not over-concerned about their sufferings and never lose courage. To conclude, look upon the eyes of the Savior who comforts them, and see how all of them together aspire to him.

3. You have already left Satan with his sad and wretched throng by way of the good affections that you have conceived. Still you have not yet joined Jesus the King, nor have you enrolled in his blessed company of devout souls, but you have always been between the two.

4. The Blessed Virgin, together with St. Joseph, St. Louis, St. Monica, and a hundred thousand others in the ranks of those living in the world invite you and encourage you.

5. The crucified King calls you by name, "Come, my well-beloved, come, that I may crown you."

ELECTION

1. O world! O abominable troop! No, never shall you see me beneath your banner! I have forever abandoned your mad, fruitless ways. King of pride, accursed king, infernal spirit, I renounce you and all your empty pomps! I detest you and all your works.

2. I turn to you, my own Jesus, King of happiness and eternal
   glory, and I embrace you with all the strength of my soul.
   I adore you with my whole heart. I choose you to be my
   King now and forever. By this inviolable act of fidelity I
   pay you irrevocable homage. I submit myself to your holy
   laws and ordinances.

3. O holy Virgin, my beloved Lady, I choose you for my
   guide. I put myself under your direction and offer you
   particular respect and special reverence. My guardian
   angel, present me to this sacred assembly. Do not forsake
   me until I have been enrolled in this blessed company.
   With them I say and I will say forever in testimony to my
   choice: Live, Jesus! Live, Jesus!

Notes

TO BEGIN

1. Francis de Sales, *Introduction to the Devout Life*, trans. John K. Ryan, 2nd ed. (New York: Image/Doubleday, 1989), 40. All citations of the *Introduction* refer to this edition.

2. *Introduction*, First part, 5.

3. Ibid., First part, 5.

4. Ibid., First part, 7.

5. Ibid., Preface.

6. Ibid., First part, 8.

7. Ibid., Second part, 2.

8. By "mystery" he means a particular concept from scripture or from the contents of the meditations.

9. *Introduction*, Second part, 7.

THE FIRST MEDITATION: ON OUR CREATION

1. *Introduction*, First part, 9.

THE SECOND MEDITATION: ON THE END FOR WHICH WE WERE CREATED

1. *Introduction*, First part, 10.

2. Ibid., First part, 10.

3. See *Introduction*, First part, 10.

4. Augustine, *Confessions*, trans. Rex Warner (New York: Signet, 2009), Book 1, Chapter 1.

5. See Thomas Aquinas, *Summa Theologica* I-II, Question 2.

6. A favorite expression of St. Francis de Sales.

7. *Introduction*, First part, 10.

THE THIRD MEDITATION: ON GOD'S BENEFACTIONS

1. *Introduction*, First part, 11.

2. Brian Kolodiejchuk, ed., *Mother Teresa: Come Be My Light* (New York: Doubleday, 2007), 225.

THE FOURTH MEDITATION: ON SIN

1. *Introduction*, First part, 12.

2. Ibid., First part, 7.

3. Ibid., First part, 7.

4. Ibid., First part, 7.

5. Ibid., First part, 8.

6. Ibid., First part, 12.

7. In Luke 7:36ff, the sinful woman bathes Christ's feet in her tears and anoints them with costly ointment.

THE FIFTH MEDITATION: ON DEATH

1. *Introduction*, First part, 13.

2. Ibid., First part, 13.

3. Graham Greene, *The Power and the Glory* (New York: Penguin Group, 2003), 210.

4. Aristotle, *Nicomachean Ethics*, Book II, 6.

5. See *Nicomachean Ethics*, Book VIII, 3.

THE SIXTH MEDITATION: ON JUDGMENT

1. *Introduction*, First part, 14.

2. St. Teresa extensively discusses mental prayer in chapter 8 of her autobiography, *Life*.

3. *Introduction*, First part, 14.

4. Ibid., First part, 14.

5. Liturgy of the Hours, Saturday of the Third Week of Lent, Office of Readings, Second Reading.

THE SEVENTH MEDITATION: ON HELL

1. *Introduction*, First part, 15.

2. Christopher McQuarrie, *The Usual Suspects*, directed by Bryan Singer (United States: Gramcery Pictures, 1995).

THE EIGHTH MEDITATION: ON PARADISE

1. *Introduction*, First part, 16.

2. "Everything that the Father gives me will come to me, and I will not reject anyone who comes to me, because I came down from heaven not to do my own will but the will of the one who sent me. And this is the will of the one who sent me, that I should not lose anything of what he gave my, but that I should raise it on the last day. For this is the will of my Father, that everyone who sees the Son and believes in him may have eternal life, and I shall raise him on the last day" (Jn 6:37–40).

THE NINTH MEDITATION: THE ELECTION AND CHOICE OF HEAVEN

1. *Introduction*, First part, 17.

2. Ibid., First part, 17.

THE TENTH MEDITATION: THE ELECTION AND CHOICE THE SOUL MAKES OF A DEVOUT LIFE

1. Ibid., First part, 18.

2. Ibid., First part, 18.

CONCLUSION

1. Ibid., Fifth part, 10.

APPENDIX: ST. FRANCIS DE SALES'S ORIGINAL MEDITATIONS

1. From Francis de Sales, *Introduction to the Devout Life*, trans. John K. Ryan, 2nd ed. (New York: Image/Doubleday, 1989), 52–71.

REV. JOHN BURNS is a priest of the Archdiocese of Milwaukee. Ordained in 2010, he has served as an associate pastor and pastor in Milwaukee as well as an adjunct professor of moral theology at the Sacred Heart Seminary and School of Theology. Burns completed a doctorate in moral theology at the Pontifical University of the Holy Cross in Rome in 2019. His doctoral research focused on the theology of healing through forgiveness.

Burns speaks at conferences, preaches missions, and directs retreats throughout the country. He is the author of *Lift Up Your Heart*. Burns works extensively with the Sisters of Life and Mother Teresa's Missionaries of Charity and has given retreats, conferences, and spiritual direction for the sisters in Africa, Europe, and the United States.

For a complete listing of titles from

Ave Maria Press

Sorin Books

Forest of Peace

Christian Classics

visit www.avemariapress.com